A FAMILY LIKE YOURS

A FAMILY LIKE YOURS

BREAKING THE PATTERNS OF DRUG ABUSE

JAMES L. SORENSEN
AND GUILLERMO BERNAL

1817

Harper & Row, Publishers, San Francisco

Cambridge, Hagerstown, New York, Philadelphia, Washington
London, Mexico City, São Paulo, Singapore, Sydney

The Twelve Traditions of Narcotics Anonymous are reprinted with permission from the World Service Office of Narcotics Anonymous. The Twelve Traditions of N.A. were adapted with permission from Alcholics Anonymous World Services Offices. The Twelve Traditions of A.A. are: 1-Our common welfare should come first; personal recovery depends on A.A. unity. 2-For our group purpose there is but one ultimate authority—a loving God as He may express Himself in our group conscience. Our leaders are but trusted servants; they do not govern. 3-The only requirement for A.A. membership is a desire to stop drinking. 4-Each group should be autonomous except in matters affecting other groups or A.A. as a whole. 5-Each group has but one primary purpose—to carry its message to the alcoholic who still suffers. 6-An A.A. group ought never endorse, finance, or lend the A.A. name to any related facility or outside enterprise, lest problems of money, property, and prestige divert us from our primary purpose. 7-Every A.A. group ought to be fully self-supporting, declining outside contributions. 8-Alcoholics Anonymous should remain forever nonprofessional, but our service centers may employ special workers. 9-A.A., as such, ought never be organized; but we may create service boards or committees directly responsible to those they serve. 10-Alcoholics Anonymous has no opinion on outside issues; hence, the A.A. name ought never be drawn into public controversy. 11-Our public relations policy is based on attraction rather then promotion; we need always maintain personal anonymity at the level of press, radio, and films. 12-Anonymity is the spiritual foundation of all our traditions, ever reminding us to place principles before personalities.

(Reprinted for adaption on page 139 with permission of A.A. World services, Inc.)

Library of Congress Cataloging-in-Publication Data
Sorensen, James L.
   A family like yours.
   Includes index.
   1. Narcotic addicts—United States—Family
relationships. 2. Narcotic addicts—Rehabilitation—
United States. 3. Drug abuse—Treatment—
United States. I. Bernal, Guillermo. II. Title.
HV5825.S585 1986   362.2'938   86-45026
ISBN 0-06-250820-2

87 88 89 90 91 HC 10 9 8 7 6 5 4 3 2 1

Contents

TABLE AND FIGURES

Preface

People who abuse drugs do not exist in a vacuum. They have families, and those families are inevitably affected. This book is for those families, and for people who want to help those families. By the time you finish reading this book you will understand how drug abuse affects families, why it happens, and how it can be stopped.

We have helped many families to cope with serious drug problems. For four years we have been leading groups of family members, helping them to get through the frequent crises, seeing how they suffer. We have taught them about drug abuse in twenty-hour "sponsor training" courses, in monthly support groups, and in family therapy. Their stories—about how drug abuse handicapped the family and about how families overcame the problem —make up the core of the book. The drug problem in many of these families was heroin addiction—a serious substance abuse disorder in which the drug "habits" of the addicted family member cost an average of $140 per day and the family's problems are intensified. This is about as bad as things can get. But family problems are the same whether one is coping with cocaine, marijuana, alcohol, or any other drug of abuse.

Recovering from drug addiction is a difficult task. But once family and community resources are marshalled, recovery is much more feasible. This book is our attempt to take people beyond conventional methods of coping with drug abuse by reaching out to those who are most concerned about the drug abuse: the family. Overcoming drug abuse is to extend the battle not only from the individual to the family, but to our communities and society as well.

This is not only a "how to" book but a "how come" book. If you worry about a relative's drug use, or if drug abuse or alcoholism seems to run in your family, or if a family member seems to have "gone wrong" and you don't know why, or if you want to comfort and help a family with a drug abuse problem—this book is for you. Families hold many of the keys that open doors to understanding drug abuse, and to sealing it off from future generations. Families can overcome drug abuse: We have seen them do it.

Acknowledgments

First, we thank the staff, patients, and families of the Mission Methadone Maintenance Treatment Program at Substance Abuse Services, San Francisco General Hospital, for their support. Without the cooperation of these experienced and brave individuals such a book would not be possible. They participated enthusiastically in both treatment and research efforts, helping to develop improved ways to treat opiate addiction. From them we learned of the courage it takes for a family to face a drug problem, and the kind of effort it takes to give up drug abuse.

We are grateful to the Treatment Research Branch of the National Institute on Drug Abuse for supporting our research on family treatment of drug abuse, through research grants to the University of California, entitled "Community Network Approach to Drug Abuse Treatment" and "Intergenerational Family Therapy with Drug Abusers." Our project officers, Frank Tims and Rebecca Ashery, helped us to think about the appropriate outlet for the ideas expressed in this book.

Much of our work in the last four years centered around the "Community Network" and "Intergenerational Family Therapy" research projects; we want to recognize the leaders of these two research teams for furthering the development of the ideas expressed in this book: Yvette Flores-Ortiz, David R. Gibson, Linda Menicucci, Carmenza Rodriguez-Dragin, and Laurie Wermuth were key team members for at least three years in these projects, and were joined by a number of dedicated staff and students.

We hold a special gratitude to several people who gave their time and energy to critique chapters in this book. We appreciate the editorial suggestions of these individuals, who include Steven Batki, Richard Chaisson, David R. Gibson, Nehoma Hirdler, Laurel and Patricia Koepernik, Michael Massing, and Laurie Wermuth.

We appreciate the help of several people who guided us on the road to publication. Although the authors have published a number of professional articles in the past, this is the first time we have written for a more general audience. Jeffrey Baker provided valuable advice early on about how to approach the task. Michael Rossi, chief psychologist at San Francisco General Hospital, provided encouragement and has been a valuable mentor to us both. Jeffrey O'Connell and Dan Skrzynski provided valuable advice and counsel about the book-publishing contract; we appreciate their skill and thorough professionalism. In addition, we thank Clayton Carlson and Steve Dietz of Harper & Row, who believed in this book and guided us through the publication process.

Finally, we appreciate the support of Laurel and Ana Isabel, our spouses, who helped us over the bumpy parts of the road and consistently encouraged us in completing this project. To them, and to our families of origin, we dedicate this book.

This book has considerable case material. In describing situations that reflect real lives, the authors altered, eliminated, and disguised information that might identify individuals, and disassociated sensitive material from them. In plain language, uncles became mothers, aunts became brothers, and so forth; in similar fashion we changed locations, sexes, ages, and so on.

Although we appreciate the support of the individuals and organizations mentioned here, the views and opinions expressed in this book are those of the authors and do not reflect the official position or policies of the University of California, San Francisco, or the National Institute on Drug Abuse.

I. THE FAMILY PERSPECTIVE

1. Overcoming Drug Abuse

You can't help people unless they are willing to be helped. I can't stress that enough. They have to want to do it, because if they don't it's like with alcoholics. You can push them, shove them, threaten them, and love them, but no way. There has to be something strong enough that's going to make them want to at least try.

Ultimately, it is the drug abuser who must win the battle with drugs. But that battle need not be fought alone. Families can help. In fact, former drug abusers most frequently cite family members as the biggest factor in their recovery.[1]

Recovered drug abusers can never get back all of the opportunities missed during the time of their addiction. Neither can family members recapture all the fresh optimism they expended during their initial efforts to help. However, drug abusers and family members can regain parts of themselves that have been buried for years. We have seen many such recoveries. It is always exciting to watch a new person emerge as the drug-oriented lifestyle is rejected in favor of living "clean."

Recovery does occur. This chapter takes a look at individuals and families who are making progress in overcoming drug abuse. Not everyone is successful: The prospects of recovery are better if the person with the drug problem has not progressed too far into drug dependence. Families are more likely to recover a sense of purpose if the drug abuse came in response to a particular problem of family life rather than in response to an accumulation of problems, and if family resources are available. No matter what the odds are, however, people do recover, and families are a key to the process.

INDIVIDUALS IN RECOVERY

Who is likely to overcome a drug problem? The 1982 national survey on drug abuse found that people who used marijuana very occasionally as teenagers were much more likely to quit as they matured, compared with those who used marijuana heavily in their teenage years. Prospects for recovery are also better if the drug abuse came about relatively recently, and if only one kind of drug was abused.[2] In short, the less people have progressed into the drug life, the greater their likelihood of getting out.

What about those who are undergoing recovery *against* the odds? We will look at people who were addicted to heroin for at least two years; the fact that they can overcome their drug abuse provides hope to people whose drug problems are less severely advanced. Their stories illustrate how drug abusers become open to change, face the issues, take more responsibility (and get more credit), as well as how friends and family can both help the drug abuser and live fuller lives themselves.

BEING OPEN TO CHANGE

I was addicted to heroin for seven years. I guess I tried methadone maintenance as a last resort. It helped, but I stayed on methadone maintenance for nine years. That was some nine years! I got married, had two kids, got divorced, found jobs, and lost jobs on methadone. I sort of tried to get off methadone, but somehow I never made a real effort. Finally I decided to go into a therapeutic community, where I stayed for eighteen months. I got off methadone in six months of treatment there. Since then I've worked for several years at a steady job and I'm doing well. I wouldn't say I'm recovered, but I'm recovering . . .

People who want to get off drugs must put themselves in a position where change becomes possible. They may ask a counselor for help or decide to enter a drug treatment program. Many times, after having repeatedly rejected it, they finally decide to take advantage of family therapy that has been available to them all along.

Sometimes the request for help is indirect. One man with a severe drug problem began to commit crimes quite openly; on later reflection, he realized that *he really wanted to get caught.* Getting taken off the streets ended up being his first step toward recovery.

FACING THE ISSUES

When we got into treatment—that was intense! It was the first time in years that Dick and I sat down and talked about the disappointment, the lying, the stealing, the fears, the hope, the sense of helplessness we've had around my drug use, some of the futility and sadness involved with it. For once we didn't blame or preach at each other.

Denial is a prime characteristic of drug abuse—denial that anything is wrong, sometimes denial of the drug abuse itself. Recovery, therefore, is marked by honestly facing the issues. Initially this can be overwhelming and painful, but the drug abuser must face the truth before permanent change is possible. We have seen many people who absolutely refuse to think about the many negative things they did when they were abusing drugs. These people seem most likely to relapse.

Most programs encourage drug abusers to take stock of their wrongdoings, so that they can overcome their guilt. For example, self-help groups like Cocaine Anonymous ask participants to admit the exact nature of their wrongs, make a list of people they have harmed, and make direct amends to them whenever possible. People in recovery take stock of themselves, do what they can to repair the damage of the past, and avoid making the same mistakes in the future:

It makes me feel good to go up to someone I "burned" back then and say: "Here, this is the money I took from you three years ago."

MORE RESPONSIBILITY, MORE CREDIT

Ken has started acting a little better . . . changed. He started trying to help me around the house, doing little things. He helped me repair my washing machine, and my iron. He even helped me paint my bathroom.

The positive effects of recovery, once begun, can grow spontaneously. A woman gets a job, and with it comes a new set of friends who are not involved with drug abuse. They may not even know of her drug history. Work occupies her time, she is praised for her job, and it has nothing to do with drugs.

In recovery, former drug abusers begin to change their idea of themselves as losers. For years they may have given up easily, half-heartedly trying to stop using drugs and then saying, "Oh, the hell with it. Life without drugs isn't worth the effort." Here is where the family can help. The change in attitude *must* come from within; the family cannot change the person's self-image. However, by expecting success instead of failure, the family can help the process:

My wife and I have been having some financial problems that involve us and my parents, and my input was valuable in the whole scheme of things. We were able to work out the whole problem, and I was able to put in a good deal of the solution. My family is reacting to me like normal people would. I didn't feel like my father was asking me: "Are you sure it's going to be all right?" We worked it out. No one looked at me like somehow I was going to sabotage the whole thing. Amazing, it was great!

SUPPORT OF FRIENDS

Sometimes friends provide a bridge that families cannot. Because friends have a relationship that is not silted up by years of family history, they can often provide a more detached view.

A person who is overcoming a drug problem can find it extremely helpful to have a friend who has not been involved in the drug world. One of our clients in the early stages of recovery was helped by a "straight" friend to find decent living in a clean motel, and then helped more by being introduced to a new circle of acquaintances who frequented a local coffee shop. Another woman, who was used to relating to people only when she was stoned, got advice from her girlfriend about how to act on breaks at the office where they worked, so that she would make friends rather than lose them. Another advantage of friends is that, compared with a family member who has been overinvolved, they may know more clearly when to stop "carrying" people in recovery and let them make their own decisions.

A friend who is a former drug abuser can also be a tremendous resource, by virtue of understanding the "street life" and what it takes to get out of it. People with drug problems can really be inspired by another person who was in the same boat, but who has made progress and cares about them:

I remind them of what it was like. I ask, "Do you have twenty dollars, or seventy dollars? That's what you would be spending on drugs." Then I suggest other ways to spend the money. We can go to a movie, or you can buy yourself something you've wanted for a long time. We can go to a concert, bowling, dancing, or just take a drive to the beach and simply talk about why you want to "use."

PROVIDING SUPPORT IN THE FAMILY

Now that I'm off drugs, I think my mother has really found herself in her own way. Her relationship with her own life and her job is better. She's getting validation for that. She feels like she's finally becoming successful at something. She's let go of me, and I feel great. She doesn't call me all the time and worry. Our relationship is adult now—aside from being her daughter, I'm a person.

People who are giving up drugs can find it helpful to see that family members are happy and don't need to worry about them. They are relieved to no longer be the center of family attention. Being out of the spotlight allows them to develop their own lives, free from disabling guilt. It can even be gratifying to be the "good one" for a change:

My parents came over to our house just to get away from the uproar at my brother's. That's a switch that I like. Now we're *the oasis of peace.*

MAKING IT WITHOUT TREATMENT

Recovery can sometimes happen without treatment. Sociologist Daniel Waldorf interviewed over one hundred former heroin addicts who "cleaned up" without treatment and had been abstinent for at least four years.[3] Some of them said that they simply grew out of heroin use. The maturation theory of drug abuse claims that the majority of people with severely disabling drug addiction develop it in their teenage years and early twenties and later simply mature out of the problem.[4]

Waldorf found that some people had, indeed, grown out of the lifestyle, but others gave up drugs in different ways. Some changed their living situation; they moved out of the drug-dealing environment and never returned to drug abuse. Some had friends who had died from overdoses, and they decided that they did not want to go out that way. Others hit rock bottom and said: "No more!" Still others hit bottom and bounced several times before giving up drugs permanently.

FAMILIES IN RECOVERY

It is not only the drug abusers who recover—their families experience recovery as well. A mother may put personal development "on hold" for years until the drug problem of her child has been overcome—or at least until the problem is less chaotic. A husband may have been so busy looking after his addicted wife that he had no time for his own problems. A family member can choose to become part of the solution, can begin to talk more openly about difficult situations, can develop family problem-solving skills, look into the family's history and losses, and help other family members to begin trusting each other again. As a family makes progress in this journey to recovery life does not become trouble free; but they can gain new perspectives on the pressures that may have prevented the family from living a fuller life.

BECOMING PART OF THE SOLUTION

My granddaughter lost her mother eight-and-a-half years ago . . . she got into the wrong crowd and I preached and lectured at her . . . I talk to her a lot. I am the grandmother and mother, 'cause she lost her mother.

When I confront my daughter and she says she hasn't done anything, I get mad because I smell it. I know when there's drugs in my house. I know that.

When one or more members are willing to help by *getting involved* in defeating drug abuse and supporting the recovery process, the family is on its way to recovery. In the 1960s it was commonly said, "If you are not part of the solution, you are part of the problem." Becoming part of the solution is essential in defeating drug abuse.

A family member alone cannot produce change but can only change his or her relationship with the drug abuser. Although everyone is accountable for changing and improving relationships, only the person abusing drugs can put an end to the misbehavior. While it is important for family members to be part of the solution, it is also important to remember that *the family is not the cause of the drug abuse.*

Furthermore, drug abuse is such a difficult and multifaceted problem that it requires not only work on the part of the individual and family members, but also efforts at the community and political levels. A family united against the abuse *can* have a powerful impact on the behavior of drug abusing family members, but these efforts will be more powerful if the family lives in a community that discourages drug abuse. To effectively combat drug abuse, a family member may need to get involved in community action with agencies such as schools.

TALKING OPENLY ABOUT PROBLEMS

Now we can sit down, talk about the problem, and come to a conclusion. We used to holler and scream at each other and never resolve anything. We've gotten to a point where we understand the only way things are going to work is if we tell each other what's going on, and work at it from there.

The prospects for recovery increase dramatically when family members are available and become part of the treatment.[5] Relatives must stop avoiding or blaming each other, and begin to talk with each other in new and different ways.

It is equally as important to have a special place to sit down, a time to talk without interruptions, a limit to the time, and someone to referee or help them talk. For families with a multiplicity of problems, the structure of a treatment program in and of itself can have beneficial effects. Having to come to appointments and having a context in which to work at resolving problems is an important step for them. As family members begin to talk openly and honestly with each other, trust, confidence, and support begin to build.

BUILDING SKILLS IN PROBLEM-SOLVING

When we came to therapy we got a plan of operation and made some commitments. . . . I am glad I went and changed my ways and met him halfway.

I don't think we really listened to each other before. I mean really listened. We'd be yelling and screaming at each other but nobody was listening. Then we would both apologize at the end for being so upset with each other, but the issue that started the argument would never be settled.

Families in therapy to overcome a drug problem report that the process has made them better able to handle problems and communicate. Having a structure for dealing with the problems is helpful, but what one does in that time is crucial. Families who develop a plan of action, practice skills, and implement the plan are well along the path of recovery from drug abuse.

Couples in recovery repeatedly note that their style of fighting has changed. Before recovery, there seemed to be no end in sight. Verbal attacks would bring on a stronger defense and counterattacks. Often after an argument they felt depleted emotionally and were left with a sense that nothing had been accomplished. They argued, they made up, but they did not solve the problem. In contrast, as they begin to practice problem-solving skills, they find a sense of accomplishment and completion.

Some of the simplest rules of communication can have important repercussions. For example, it can be useful to agree not to interrupt each other and listen to what the other says. This can help to develop and maintain respect and dignity in relationships. Families must learn to give all members the time to state their case and come to some kind of resolution.

By the mile, life is a trial. By the yard, life is hard. But by the inch, life is a cinch.

This was the recommendation of John, who was sponsoring his son in treatment. To the recovering drug abuser, even the small problems of daily life can be overwhelming. John and his son had learned to break down problems into smaller pieces so that they could manage one piece at a time. Families on the road to recovery learn to identify each problem, come up with alternative solutions, and later implement the most workable solution.

Nobody thought we could finish the program, but we did finish it. We came to all ten sessions. It's not easy to come to these sessions week after week.

This family was proud of having completed the ten-week therapy program they set out for themselves. The ability to take one problem at a time and solve it can lead family members to build on their success and tackle larger and more difficult problems later on.

OWNING FAMILY HISTORY

Doing the family tree got me thinking about my family a lot. After that session, we organized a family reunion. I got together with relatives that I hadn't seen for years. I found out that I have about eight new grandchildren.

I saw his parents as regular people. We were relieved and they were relieved that after so many years we got together. I actually liked his father and mother . . .

It takes a great deal of courage to look at family history—particularly if the history has been problematic. Making a family tree, as discussed in Chapter 4, can help family members begin to accept and personalize their heritage. As with the man quoted above, working on drawing the family tree can sometimes stimulate family reunions.

Owning one's family history often means facing difficult relationships. Families in recovery know that working to improve relationships can have beneficial effects. A couple in marital therapy for the husband's heroin addiction noted that therapy had helped the relationships between his wife, his mother, and him:

My parents are reacting like normal people would. My husband has been a big part of the change. His relationship with my father, for instance. He never lets my father get to him. My father is finally treating my husband like an equal.

FACING LOSSES

We never talked about the death of the baby before. She was our firstborn. I could only talk about it when I was drunk. She would always blame me for her death because I didn't take her to the hospital soon enough.

When families begin to acknowledge together the importance of losses and their feelings connected to these losses, they begin to improve. Families with a drug-abusing family member tend to have many early losses and premature separations. Facing the loss and the pain connected to the loss is an important activity for families in recovery.

Guilt and overwhelming feelings of sadness can lead some family members to seek a substance that will numb these feelings. Facing the sadness, examining the impact of the loss, and mourning the loss can be important in recovery. In the example cited above, the therapist worked out a plan for the family to commemorate and acknowledge the death of their firstborn as a way to help them mourn her death and express their sadness in a nondestructive way.

BUILDING TRUST IN RELATIONSHIPS

I've been asking her to come to therapy for years and now she did it. She followed through. This helps me to trust her.

Before she was always out running around. Now she can spend time with our son. The whole household is different. She's also closer to my mother now. Before, my mother and the rest of the family were not too eager to see her because things would "disappear." Now she and my mother are doing things together regularly, and with our son too.

During the recovery process, as family members begin to acknowledge each other's efforts and struggles, trust builds slowly but naturally. Mutual recognition of what each gives and receives in a close relationship is an important step toward building trust. They work toward a balance between debts and credits in their relationships.

For example, one family in therapy began to examine how the wife had helped her husband during his difficult five-year heroin addiction. Marie cared for Bob during this time, and she "stuck by him." As he improved the couple entered therapy, where they began to talk about imbalances of fairness in their relationship. The following dialogue shows how they began to achieve a balance of fairness and trust:

Bob: *One of the things I've been fighting with is that I knew she was going to resent me, and so was our boy eventually. She was going to hate me. My fear was that we were going to spend five years with me being clean and her paying me back for how I'd treated her. I didn't think I could survive it.*

                 What I was afraid of was that she was going to pay me back by making me feel all she felt for the five years that I was dirty . . . When I started to clean up my act, I started getting resentful. I was feeling that I was getting clean and now she's starting to kill me. . . .

Therapist: *Marie, I think you are entitled to some things from him, by virtue of what you have been giving him and your child. You deserve to have certain things from him and should get them. The issue is what and how you are going to collect from him in a way that is fair.*

Marie: *Part of it is that I have to deal with my resentment. I have a real problem when I see the same kind of things cropping up again. I feel I deserve to have some of the promises made good, have him live up to and stick to them . . . like staying clean, being honest with me, working together, and not protecting me from his problems.*

Bob: *I feel I've begun paying her back by being more of those things . . . When I met her, she was working two jobs and dealing with my drug abuse, which is incredible. Now, she's going to school, and I'm working in a hardware store. She'll be able to finish school and get her degree . . .*

GAINING A NEW PERSPECTIVE

Coming here once a week gave us a chance to see ourselves objectively. I feel a sense of accomplishment. Just being able to come and talk is beneficial.

Some families find that having an objective third party to help them with their discussions can be quite helpful. In the situation described above the family was having extreme difficulty with internal fighting and emotional reactions to one another. They gained a more objective perspective by having their discussions videotaped and then examining the videotape calmly.

I used to think about the problem as my problem, my thing. I was going to handle it. Now, coming here, I see it more as a family thing. We talked about my family, her family. I also started to call on family members. We are not as alone as before.

There was a heavy sense of family. My grandmother stressed family . . . that carried over to me.

Families in recovery often gain a new sense of family pride. Family members who may have felt shame about an alcoholic father, or guilt about what could have been done but was not, discover pride in their relationships. It then becomes easier for them to reconnect with their family, overcome distrust, and support each other. This can have powerful repercussions:

I just heard about my father. He has been sober for about nine months. My father has stopped before for a month or two, but never this long. I couldn't believe it. My sister said that my Mom has been using me as an example at home. I guess she figures if I can do it, my father can too.

My wife has gotten closer to her mother and family. She sees her mother very often— this is part of her schedule for herself—and they have gotten closer again like they used to be. She has also gotten closer to her brother again.

Improved family relations often accompanies recovery. When the drug is removed, the drug abuser and the family members are able to reestablish closer ties. Relationships are also healthier as family members get a better handle on difficult and sometimes overwhelming emotions.

It is most gratifying to see how individuals and families who were isolated reconnect. Reestablishing family ties can also help one view problems in a broader framework. The point is not to blame oneself or one's family. Rather, one should gain a realistic view of the struggles, efforts, and pressures that may have handicapped everyone involved.

PROBLEMS DO NOT DISAPPEAR

Life will never be problem-free. Problems do not go away just because people are overcoming drug abuse. Families on the road to recovery know this fact and are committed to the struggle. When they work on relationships from the family perspective, they attack one problem at a time and build on small successes.

Gradually, they solve today's problems and trade them in for a new problem set:

Things have been pretty uneventful . . . I started working. This ten-week program was helpful. We ironed out some problems. It got us through summer. I think we are better able to deal with other problems now.

IMPROVING THE PROSPECTS OF RECOVERY

Recovering from drug abuse is a difficult struggle, both for the drug-dependent individual and for the family. Not everyone is able to recover, but a number of people do eventually make it back into a drug-free world. Many are able to recover with the help of family and friends, some make good use of the service provided by professionals, and a very small number recover without substantial help from anyone.

Recovery from drug abuse does not happen overnight—it is a process. For some this process may be relatively brief, while for others it may take a lifetime. From the family point of view, completing the recovery process may even take more than one generation.

People are on their way to recovery when they are more open to change, get beyond denial, start to confront difficult issues head on, and take increasing responsibility. Friends and family members can recognize these signs and lend crucial support right from the beginning.

It is in the family's best interest to get involved and become part of the solution. At the most basic level one can begin to become part of the solution by learning about drug abuse and its consequences. Next one can learn about the types of drug abuse treatment available and, perhaps, participate as a concerned family member. If deeper involvement is a possibility, one can get involved with community action—work with community groups, participate in family support meetings, and learn of associations oriented toward preventing drug abuse in the community.

HOW TO USE THIS BOOK

Recovery can occur, and family members are the key to it. Well-guided action of family and friends can go a long way toward breaking the patterns of drug abuse.

Part I (Chapters 1 through 4) presents information about how families overcome and struggle with the problems of drug abuse. Part II (Chapters 5 and 6) tells how to practice principles of family survival and change. Part III (Chapters 7 through 10) explores the resources aimed at providing basic information on drug abuse, its treatment, and the family.

This book contains a number of principles that may be helpful to the family in overcoming drug problems. An important part of the battle is to gain understanding of the situation. Chapters 2 through 4 focus on how families often unwittingly get caught in the middle of drug-abuse problems. Chapter 2 illustrates how families become and remain involved in drug abuse and how they can assist in recovery. Chapter 3 discusses the stages of life that all families go through, and how drug use is involved at each stage. For example, drug abuse frequently becomes a problem when a family has adolescent children, and it can be worse when family members cannot let go of each other.

Chapter 4 presents the intergenerational view—drug abuse can be invisibly tied to previous generations. For example, a boy named John, who is the spitting image of his alcoholic Uncle John, may have been treated for years as if he has the same kinds of difficulties as his namesake. The boy may then react by "acting out" the legacy, turning into his generation's "bad Uncle John." Every person is caught up in a web of family history. *It's nobody's fault, but everybody can help in recovery.*

The second part of the book shows how families can change their relationships to overcome the problems of drug abuse. Chapter 5 suggests several approaches, and illustrates the principle that *we take roles and can change them for new roles.*

Chapter 6 concerns motivation. How can a family member help

the drug abuser to say "no"? How can the family help the drug abuser to try harder at living a normal life? *One cannot change the motivation of drug abusers, but one family member can change their personal relationship with them.*

The third part of the book is designed as a resource for family members and for people who work with families in which there is a drug problem. Chapter 7 tells how to recognize the signs of drug abuse. It is based on our belief that *denial doesn't help.* Chapter 8 explains the different kinds of drug treatment that are available, both for family members and for drug abusers. *Drug abuse is a complicated disorder; no single action can change everything.* To help deal with the various facets of addiction, it is helpful to know the treatment options that are available, how to use them, and how they can be misused.

Chapter 9 provides information on the alarming problem of Acquired Immunodeficiency Syndrome (AIDS), its link to drug abuse, and its impact on the family. Learning about AIDS can help families to be instrumental in preventing the spread of AIDS among drug abusers and their loved ones.

Chapter 10 presents specific resources that can provide a family member with help or information.

Each reader will use this book differently. To understand the ingredients needed to overcome drug abuse among family members, we recommend that you begin with Part I. If you are particularly interested in combating drug abuse by making family changes, Part II (Chapters 5 and 6) may be most useful. If your questions focus more on how and where to get help or support, Part III provides a diagnostic and resource guide.

It is in the best interest of most families to learn as much about drug abuse as they can. Families have the same kinds of problems, whether or not they are troubled by drug abuse. The differences are a matter of degree. People who have a problem with drugs are in need of family and friends who understand. They need an ally in their efforts to change, and their most effective ally can be the family. Likewise, the family member needs support when someone close has a drug problem. In this way knowledgeable friends and professionals can be very helpful. Ultimately, it will be in the interest of future generations to put a stop to drug abuse. By preventing the development of further problems, families will break the patterns of drug abuse.

2. How Drug Abuse Happens in Families

FAMILIES CAUGHT UP IN THE DRUG PROBLEM

GETTING BEYOND DENIAL

I come from a small town in the South, and there is no drug history in my family. My husband has a problem, though. It took me a long time to find out about Neil's addiction. . . . I don't know when he first "used." One time I gave him rent money to pay the landlady. Three weeks later the landlady asked me for the rent. Instead of telling her what happened, I just said that I would give her the money. So I called my bank in Georgia, where I had some money, and I paid the rent.

I was really blind to what was going on. Sometimes he would come home half-conscious . . . he looked different, his eyes were glassy, but I just didn't get it. Our bank account was always overdrawn, because he would use the money machine card and not record it anywhere. Our boy didn't have new shoes to start school with. We were having to borrow money, even when I was working a night job.

Then suddenly the bubble burst. But still, he's not a regular drug addict, I know. And I can't bring myself to believe that he was hanging out with junkies.

It can take the family a long time to come to grips with the fact that one of its members has a drug problem. At first they may not notice the problem; later they deny it and cover it up in front of others. Underneath it all family members may be confused, perhaps ashamed, asking, "Why did this happen to me?" Although they tend to isolate themselves, families with a drug abuse problem need not be ashamed, nor hesitant to seek help.

PEOPLE IN TROUBLE

It's one thing to have a problem myself, and it's another to help a friend. But it really is hard, helping someone in your family that's abusing. I'm going through this with my children. At first I saw there was use, *but now I'm seeing* abuse. *I confronted them with that, but they're heavy into denial.*

They're into drinking and a little bit of cocaine, but I'm seeing this use turn into abuse, and with my own children. It's very, very difficult for me to be really confrontive. With outsiders I can easily say, "Listen, I think your drug use is getting into abuse." Then I'd help them as much as referring them to programs, we would do things together, or introduce them to other "clean" people.

My friends I can confront, but with my children it's too delicate a situation for me. I'm getting all nervous even thinking about it.

After a concerned family member has overcome denial—has admitted a problem exists—it is still difficult to discuss the issues with the person who is abusing drugs. The man quoted above had worked with drug abusers in treatment programs for many years and was respected as an ex-addict who knew how to help people. However, when it came to dealing with his own family, he felt handcuffed emotionally.

When a family member has a drug problem, the difficulties are compounded because the problem is so close. The family member is turned inside out: "Is it my fault? What if the relatives find out? Can my own kin *really* have a problem that bad?" The feelings become so intense that it is difficult to think clearly about the problem, much less how to help the family come to terms with it.

I used to come home and see her asleep on the sofa in front of the television, after I'd been working all day. I think a lot of that was just plain escape because she hadn't done much and felt bad about it, and she didn't want to be conscious.

For some, drug use is a way to experience intense feelings that they have somehow lost the capability to experience without drugs.[1] No matter what the reason, the majority of people with a severe drug problem suffer from depression.[2] Confronting the problem requires courage on both sides in the family—both the family and the drug user can have emotional blocks.

When a family member has a drug problem, everyone suffers. The user feels guilty, upset, and out of control. Parents feel guilty, furious, or both. Brothers and sisters may resent the person with the problem. Children wonder if *they* are going to become drug abusers. The entire family feels troubled. Most of all, each individual feels guilty, and guilt is the enemy of change. For a family to overcome a problem with drugs, individual family members must first overcome their own feelings of inadequacy about dealing with the problem.

In our work with families of heroin addicts we have seen a hundred families that do not understand how to overcome the drug problem. They need information, they need to learn and practice family communication techniques, and they need to forgive themselves.

COMMUNICATION

I've tried everything with him. I've tried getting mad, I've tried being supportive, but nothing works. I'll listen to him. Try to be supportive. When I use any type of negative approach, he immediately gets outraged and just cuts me off completely. If we're on the phone he'll hang up; person-to-person he'll walk out. He just won't listen. He's beyond listening.

Change is difficult when communication is one-sided. Sometimes even the people closest to the drug user feel that they are not getting through. The person doing the talking begins to feel like a nag; the person being talked to begins to feel like a child. The pattern continues until the topic changes, or one or both parties change the way they communicate.

I'll listen to my brother. I try to help him that way because he can't go to my mother, because my mother can't. She cries, she gets upset, she gets nervous, she gets sick. She can't handle him. She wonders how her two sons could turn out so different from each other. So mainly I try to listen to him.

We all take on roles in life. In families, roles often become set. For example, in many families one person takes major family responsibility. Like the brother who is quoted above, the "strong one" takes on tasks that others cannot handle. But where there is strength there is also weakness, and the family that has one member in the strong role will usually have another member in the weak role.

In a marriage one spouse may take care of life's problems for the couple, while the other allows himself or herself to be taken care of. Another frequent pattern is that of pursuer-distancer. In this pattern the "pursuer" continually tries to get close to the other person, the "distancer," who tries to maintain a greater space between them.

It is difficult to change these patterns—for the weak one to show strength or for the strong one to show weakness; for the pursuer to stop chasing or for the distancer to turn around and begin to close the gap. Change requires skilled alteration of the relationship—family members must continue to have their needs met, while stepping out of their old dissatisfying roles.

In terms of being educated about how to deal with somebody who uses drugs, I've been dealing with it for ten years, and I still don't know how to deal with it. I don't know how to say, "What's that mark on your arm? Is that a scratch or what?" I don't know how to say it in a way that won't cause a big fight.

We get so used to reacting in a certain way that we forget there can be other ways to handle a problem. *Families often get stuck in their patterns of relating.* To get unstuck, family members must realize first that there are alternative approaches to their methods of communication. Using new approaches can catapult everyone in the family into new worlds of understanding.

SECRETS AND BURDENS

COVERING UP

I had to cover everything up for my husband. He was on cocaine, and then he was in the detox program. But then he went back to cocaine again. He only used the treatment time to get enough money to go back to drugs. In the meantime a gang was knocking at my door, and there were other people asking me for the money that Steven owed them. Finally, Steven was thrown in jail. One time I was at my brother's house preparing for their anniversary, and I had to tell them that Steven was sick. "Oh, he's got the flu and can't leave the house." Really, he was in jail for the next two months!

Family members sometimes cover up the drug problem as a way to protect the person with the problem or as a way to protect themselves from embarrassment and pain. When the problem is alcoholism, this behavior is called "co-alcoholic," and in drug abuse such a person is called a "co-addict." Although some amount of protection is reasonable, co-addicts actually alter their lifestyle to cover up for the drug abuser. This extent of covering up not only changes the life of the family member, but it *makes it easy for the abuser to stay addicted.* To get out of this pattern requires learning to *not* do for addicts what they ought to be able to do for themselves. This lets them suffer the consequences of their actions.

TRYING TO LIVE A NORMAL LIFE

Families adapt to the stress of a drug problem just as they adapt to illness or death of family members, financial hardship, or countless other disruptions of normal family life. They make adjustments. "I try not to worry about it, but put it in the Lord's hands," says one father. A wife of a drug abuser works two jobs to maintain the family's standard of living, because her husband hasn't been working since he began "using." A husband describes how he adapted their social life:

It would always feel uncomfortable having other people over to our apartment. It felt like it was a real invasion of her privacy, and I thought it was an invasion of my social life too, that I couldn't have friends over when she was busy running around dealing with getting high. She was embarrassed for people to see her, and so she would hide because she was embarrassed. She felt like I didn't want to be associated with her around my friends.

THE CHILDREN'S DIFFICULTIES

Children of substance abusers have a particularly difficult time. They tend toward caution and suspicion as youngsters, and toward self-doubt as they mature. Sometimes one will be raised as a "parentified child"—a role reversal in which the child takes care of his or her parents.

In our drug treatment program each person who begins treatment has a "sponsor"—a family member or friend not involved in drug abuse who is willing to help the client in recovery. We hold monthly support group meetings for clients and sponsors together, and periodically we offer a twenty-hour sponsor-training workshop.

In our program Carl was unusual in that he sponsored both of his parents in treatment. Both Vic and Suzanne had been addicted to drugs for years, yet they raised Carl to be a wonderful son. He was the strong one in the family, encouraging his parents to get in treatment. When asked what he wanted from treatment, he replied, "I guess I just want to be proud of them, to say 'my parents were addicts once, but they aren't anymore.' " In one session we asked clients what the family could do for them. Vic and Suzanne wanted Carl to tell them about jobs. Carl explained why that would be difficult: "It would be easier if you weren't my father. For me to say, 'Oh, he's my father,' that would be harder than, 'That's my friend, and he needs a job.' "

HOSPITALS AND HOPE

Sometimes treatment for drug abuse holds a family together.[3] For example, many times a family will rally around the drug abuser once the problems have become so serious that he or she is hospitalized. Similarly, the husband of one applicant to our program was ready to leave his wife, but he agreed to stay if she would go into treatment.

Other times, curiously, the drug abuse itself holds a family together. For example, a teenager's drug abuse can give the parents a problem to focus on, whereas without it they would drift apart or be in conflict. The drawback in this situation is that recovery from drug abuse can act as a destabilizing force, yielding more problems for the family. So the family has a dual problem with the drug abuse: The only way they can unite is when there is a drug problem, but everyone resents it.

WAITING FOR THE OTHER SHOE TO DROP

My husband is working now, but he feels it's not good enough for him and might quit. No matter what the job, it's better now because before his whole day was focused on drugs. I'm worried that he'll just quit working. I'm terrified that he'll quit, and the bottom will fall out.

During rehabilitation family members walk on eggshells around the recovering addict, fearing the worst. How much pressure should they put on their loved one, who seems to be trying to make it? One mother says it this way:

The hard thing is that I don't really want to confront her to the point where she'll really mess up. I'm afraid that when I'm accusing her of something, she'll really get mad at me and really go heavily into it. So I'm treating it with kid gloves.

Family members often try to "walk softly" by suggesting alternative activities to drug use, but this also puts pressure on the family. "It's hard to distract my boyfriend," says the lover of one of our clients. "I can do it for a day or night, but that's all. I never know what's going on in his life." In short, the family members who care about the person with the drug problem often live in constant fear that their loved one will relapse.

I CAN'T AFFORD TO BE OPTIMISTIC

Even the most competent family members may feel paralyzed when trying to deal with substance abuse. The drug abuser turns quietly inward, hiding from the family and from himself or herself. Members cannot cope effectively while they feel guilty. Communication patterns are mixed up. Some family members become caretakers of the drug abuser, while the family protects other members from the problem. Nobody knows how to get out of communication patterns that are not working. To live a normal life, the family may cover up the problem or try to deny it. Children suffer. Sometimes the only time of hope is when the person's health deteriorates so badly that he or she needs hospitalization. Finally, the family lives in fear of the drug user's next "run" or binge.

The family may sometimes need to be skeptical:

I was always optimistic before about my daughter, but now I'm not optimistic. Not because I don't want to be. No, I just don't want to be conned. When I'm optimistic, I feel a little conned.

JUDGING THE EXTENT OF THE PROBLEM

How can the family assess whether or not it has a problem? In our treatment program we ask about the severity of problems caused by the drug abuse. Our Family Difficulties Checklist can help a person to identify the extent of the problem:

What difficulties has the family been experiencing with drug abuse? In the past thirty days, to what extent were these a problem for the family?

1. The drug user's poor health worried or caused problems for the family.
2. The drug user borrowed money or strained family finances.
3. The family had problems with the drug user's alcohol abuse.
4. The drug user's legal troubles worried or caused problems for the family.
5. The drug user's illegal activities created problems for the family.
6. The drug user did not take care of family responsibilities.
7. The family saw less of the drug user than it would have liked.
8. The drug user brought undesirable people home.
9. The drug user's drug abuse limited the family's social activities.
10. The drug user had serious arguments or disagreements with a family member.

11. The drug user's emotional state worried or caused problems for the family.
12. The drug user's drug abuse created distrust with family members.
13. There was physical violence between the drug user and a family member.

Important emotional issues underlie these specific questions. Do family members find themselves trying to justify their feelings and behavior? Are they burdened by taking over family responsibilities that used to belong to the person using drugs? Is the family beginning to withdraw from friends and outside activities? Do family members feel they must cover up the drug use? Do some family members feel more negatively then others about the person using drugs? Do people in the family find that many of their thoughts revolve around the drug use? Are they losing sleep worrying about it? These are signs of a family troubled by drug abuse.

FAMILIES RECOVERING FROM DRUG ABUSE

Families do not need to stay caught up in the drug problem; they can be part of the recovery process. Families can help rebuild trust, and they can help motivate the drug abuser. Working together, the family can move toward better communication. It is not easy and not always attractive—sometimes people in recovery are less exciting to be around—they are less entertaining, less unpredictable. Nevertheless, families can be of tremendous assistance in helping the person to avoid relapse. They need to be patient, realizing that recovery is a slow process and not entirely under anyone's control. Finally, family members need to keep in mind that they are not alone. Many really good people and good families have been troubled by drug abuse.

A NEW PERSONALITY IS EMERGING

I'm surprised to see a part of my husband's personality come out that I've not seen before, and that's one of the interesting parts for me. He's more able to cope with reality, and things that before he just got too upset to cope with, he can.

When people give up using drugs genuine recovery can occur. They regain parts of themselves that have been absent for years. This recovery of emotions and skills is exciting.

A person who has been troubled by drug abuse for many years, and who has failed at half-hearted attempts to give it up, loses faith in his or her ability to change. This rapidly becomes an attitude of hopelessness that contributes to the inability to give up drugs. But when such a person begins to experience even a small victory, something happens. Things begin to turn around and gather momentum. The person begins to believe in himself or herself, for the first time in a long while. We have seen people at this point change deeply and permanently. They may have given up not only drugs, but alcohol and cigarettes; or they may have undergone a religious conversion. They get excited about their own potential. For the family this is exciting, strange, and wonderful to witness.

SELF-DETERMINATION, NOT ESCAPE

I really think, at least in my son's case, he had to make up his mind. You can't force it, no matter what you do, cajole, be supportive, yell at him or anything else. It's not going to do any good until he makes up his mind.

I think I suspected for years. I knew a while back for several years that he was abusing, but I didn't know that his wife did it. That was shocking. But they just came over one Sunday morning. They told me the truth and said they wanted to get off of it. They told me about this program, asked me if I would be their sponsor. So it was their decision.

Family members often need to keep in mind that the drug abuse is not their fault, and it is not their responsibility. We tell our groups of family members to remember that "it's *their* life, not yours. Don't feel that it's your responsibility to wrench them out of a neighborhood or to heal their scars of a bad childhood. It can't be done. There is only one person who can make them change. We don't live in their shoes: We can't prevent it if they really want to get worse; and if they really want to get better we couldn't stop them if we tried. Don't feel that you must walk on eggshells."

SETTING CONDITIONS

Now I think my husband wants more things from life, and he realizes that if he doesn't go get them he won't have them. One of them is me, one of them is a family, and one of them is a career. So I think he's realized he can't have both drugs and those things.

During the recovery process, family members can help by setting limits. They make it clear, as the woman above does, that the substance abuser needs to make choices between them and drugs. Having both is not possible. One wife of a substance abuser decided to separate from her husband to graphically demonstrate that his drug use was a problem. Her method was to confront him, but also to stick by him if he would try. This approach may seem cruel at times, but it can help to have clear limits. As the husband of one substance abuser said to us: "Sometimes she asks me for something just so that I can say no."

MOTIVATION

My son and I went to one of those meetings for sponsors. There was this one woman who had been using for ten years. She said you have to put as much energy into staying straight as you used to put into getting high. That was a good message. She was saying if you used to work sixteen hours a day trying to get your money together and trying to run around to get your dope, then you should spend sixteen hours a day doing whatever it takes to live clean.

That's what I'd like to see for us. We want to put more energy into getting to a place where that woman was at.

Once the person with the drug problem has become motivated to change, the family can enjoy being part of the improvement process. On one hand it is rewarding to have the user more available to do daily chores than he or she used to be. A family member can help by expecting the drug abuser to complete these tasks, rather than being prepared for the person not to do it and being surprised when the job gets done. On the other hand, the family should not be impatient—genuine recovery takes time:

I feel like my daughter is doing a lot more than she used to do, yet I feel bad because she's still not doing half of what you expect a normal person to do. She can take care of things and get them done if pointed out, instead of putting them off, but she's not where she can look around and see what needs to be done and just get it done. So she's more into doing things, although there's still a gap there.

BETTER COMMUNICATION

Patterns of communication can change during recovery, and certain patterns need to change. For example, when the husband is a drug abuser the couple may have been interacting more like child and parent than like husband and wife. He provides the excitement, she the stability. His role may have been to get into dangerous situations, while hers was to pull him out of those situations. When the husband gives up the drug world, his role changes and so does the relationship. If the couple still relates as child and parent, however, it will be easy for him to relapse into drug abuse.

My son is beginning to readjust his body to get up in the morning, and we communicate a little better. Plus he gets up, and he goes and takes care of business. Go do this and go do that, and by one o'clock he's accomplished a lot of things, whereas before he would just be getting up. I think he's more in sync with the rest of the working world.

During recovery the drug abuser becomes more available to the family and, as the father said in the quote above, more "in sync" with the rest of the world. Generally families are relieved and happy to have the person back. But unless communication patterns change, both the family and the drug abuser can feel at loose ends: "What do I do with him now that he's around the house so much?" Or for the drug abuser: "I feel like I'm underfoot. Do they really want me to be living 'clean' with them?"

YOU GET A NORMAL PERSON

You know he's got a lot of charisma. Actually, when he was high I didn't dislike him. Now what I'm beginning to see is that sometimes he doesn't seem as if he has as much charm and personality, probably because that was all false. It might have been to compensate for the fact that he wasn't making it, or to make him acceptable. Now what I'm seeing is just the regular person. He may not be the center-stage kind of person that he presented himself as before.

On the whole, the family is greatly relieved when drug abusers give up their old lifestyle, but there is also a sense of diminished excitement. The drug abuser becomes more conventional, more responsible. No more are there late-night phone calls or early evening jaunts out of the house for an unknown time. As these habits disappear, family members should remember that the drug abusers are giving up one area and trying to join a new world where they may or may not succeed. They may not show the old sense of bravado, but instead be unsure of themselves. Most families would much rather have them this way—not as charismatic, but much more able to give and receive love.

FAMILY SUPPORT IN AVOIDING RELAPSE

I try to give my son-in-law some ideas about how to be a good parent. I'm sensitive about not being a nag, but he comes from a family of drug abusers, and Dad was an alcoholic. He really doesn't know a lot about parenting. So while I give hints, I try to give him credit for how well he's doing at giving up drugs and taking care of his children.

Family support can be crucial in preventing relapse. One study found that the principal difference between people who stayed abstinent from drugs five years after leaving a drug treatment program and those who relapsed was that those who stayed abstinent tended to have more family support.[4]

People who have given up drugs may have a lot to learn about the nondrug world. Previously they may have avoided worrying about things like punctuality, job options, or planning. It can be very helpful to *have someone on their side* who can give them hints about how to prosper in the drug-free world. Brothers and sisters may be especially effective, because their advice is likely to be viewed as helpful rather than controlling.

The family can also help by giving credit when it is due. The person in recovery may be contributing to the household in a way that would have been impossible when drugs were involved. It is valuable for the family to recognize productive, useful activities.

A family can help as much by receiving as it can by giving. Because stopping the use of drugs is such a difficult task, the person trying it needs to be able to talk with people about what's going on. Family members can help simply by being approachable —available to listen to what the drug abuser is going through. They can also encourage the drug abuser to join recovery-oriented groups of ex-addicts like Cocaine Anonymous or Narcotics Anonymous (Chapter 10 explains how to contact these and other self-help groups). Remember, however, that *being helpful by receiving requires that a family member be able to wait:*

The meetings help him talk and listen to other person's problems, and that's what he needs. He needs someone to listen and someone to talk to. That's the way I help him, by listening. I have patience.

BALANCING PATIENCE WITH EXPECTATIONS

"Can I help more by being patient or by setting standards that I think are realistic?" The answer is an ambiguous "both." Family members need to be unflappably patient while the person is making progress, realizing that recovery takes time. One woman we know waits for her daughter to do her share of the housework rather than doing it for her, but she waits in a way that is supportive: "I got up this morning and there were yesterday's dishes. But I didn't feel like it was my responsibility. Jeanie will do it." Patience does not help to solve many problems directly, but it is a way for people to show that they are on the side of people with the drug problem, rather than against them.

On the other hand, patience has some drawbacks. Drug abusers often interpret "kindness" as "weakness" and will exploit people who show only their soft side. Further, an emphasis on accomplishment *can* solve problems directly. The family member who sets real expectations can be preparing the drug abuser to succeed in the nondrug world. The woman mentioned above who waited for her daughter to do the dishes says, "She's a good mother, but she's inconsistent. I'm afraid that when she moves out on her own again, unless she changes her habits now, her apartment is going to be dirty." The key, then, is knowing at any point whether the drug abuser needs a prod or a hug. "When in doubt," we tell families, "show patience as long as you can afford it."

GOOD PEOPLE WITH A PROBLEM

I've met a lot of people that I really like who are addicts. It's a shame, because addicts are stigmatized. They don't get an edge on getting it together, they get an edge on not getting it together because of people's concepts. I can understand why people feel that way, why they don't want an addict around. They turn around and find their jewelry is gone or whatever. By conditioning they expect it. But there are a lot of really good people with this problem.

Families tend to feel alone when drug abuse is a problem. They isolate themselves because of guilt, shame, pride, or for the many other reasons discussed earlier in this chapter. However, it is a fact that family members can help the person attempting to recover from drug abuse, and family members can be a tremendous resource to each other. A family member needs to be willing to learn, and to come out from behind the wall of isolation that has built up over years of drug abuse. It can be helpful to keep in mind the words of the family member quoted above: "There are a lot of really good people with this problem."

3. Stages of Family Life and Drug Abuse

Understanding the life stages that families go through can be useful in understanding drug abuse. For example, drug use by a rebellious adolescent is usually tied to issues of leaving home, and alcohol abuse can occur in response to the loss of an aging parent.

Every family is constantly growing, developing, maturing, and adapting to its environment. Some develop better than others. How and in what ways families develop is the subject of this chapter. We offer a family developmental framework[1] for understanding the relationship between drug abuse and the life span of the family. This framework has been found useful by professionals who work with families with a wide range of mental health and drug abuse problems. The family developmental approach may orient members to the kinds of stresses and difficulties most families experience at different stages in the life cycle. Drug abuse problems often reflect the difficulties experienced by various family members in mastering specific tasks at one or another stage of development.

Table 1 charts five stages of family life, beginning with marriage and ending with the integration of loss. The left-hand column identifies the ceremony, task, conflicts, problems, and ages associated with each stage. The table draws upon the seminal conceptual work of Michael Solomon,[2] as well as later contributions on the lifecycle framework by Elizabeth Carter and Monica McGoldrick,[3] and Mark Karpel and Erick Strauss.[4] The table will serve as a basis for our discussion throughout this chapter.

Just like individuals, families grow and mature. We can think of this growth in *stages,* that is, designated periods of time through which most families pass. When and how a particular family goes

TABLE 1
STAGES OF FAMILY LIFE

	Stage I	Stage II	Stage III	Stage IV	Stage V
	Coupling	Parenthood	Children Growing up	Departure of Children	Integration of Loss
Ceremony	Matrimony	Baptism	Bar mitzvah, Confirmation	Graduation	Funerals
Task	(1) Moving away from family of origin ("cutting apron strings")	Balance marital and parental responsibilities	Parents let go of child	Parents become couple again (grandparents)	Adult children assume some responsibility for parents
	(2) Commitments to forming a new family	Solidify marriage	Child lets go of parents	Adult children live independently (new family)	Mourning losses
Conflicts	(1) Loyalty conflicts with inlaws vs. new family and clarifying new roles	Conflicts of interests between spouse and children	Separation	Individuality	Incomplete mourning
	(2) "I'm going home to Mother" syndrome	"Who comes first?" syndrome	"Who's in charge?" syndrome	"Empty nest" syndrome	

TABLE 1 *(Continued)*

	Stage I	Stage II	Stage III	Stage IV	Stage V
	Coupling	Parenthood	Children Growing up	Departure of Children	Integration of Loss
Ceremony	Matrimony	Baptism	Bar mitzvah, Confirmation	Graduation	Funerals
Problems	(1) Overinvolvement of one spouse with parent against other spouse	Marriage neglected as one spouse becomes too devoted to child rearing	Parent and child overinvolvement (binding)	Too much parental involvement or child dependence	Overattachment to one surviving member
	(2) Rejection of family of origin: "We're moving to California!"	Children neglected as parents become overly devoted to the marriage		Children pushed out too early to make it on their own	Inability to emotionally invest in new relationship due to avoidance of mourning
Ages of Children	Couples with no children	Families with preschool children (ages 1 to 6)	Families with teenage children (ages 7 to 17)	Families with young adults (ages 18 to 28)	Families with aging parents and adult children (ages 29 and over)

through a designated stage varies considerably, but generally it is necessary to go through each stage. Just as it is not possible to leap over childhood or adolescence, most stages of family life cannot be avoided.

Each stage signals an important life event, that is, a particular occurrence unique to that stage of development. Important life events usually have significant *ceremonies,* rituals that acknowledge transitions in life: marriage (weddings), childbirth (baptisms), growing up (bar mitzvahs), leaving home (graduations), and deaths (funerals). With each event the family needs to readjust to new demands on the family. In a way, each new event represents a crisis for the family. The extent to which the family is able to reorganize as it faces the demands of the current crisis will determine whether or not problems develop. The essential *task* of the family is to handle these crises at the different stages. On the one hand, this requires stability and family unity. The reality of change, on the other hand, means that the family must be flexible enough to reorganize itself. At each stage there are predictable *conflicts* that need to be resolved. If the family does not cope well, predictable *problems* will emerge, some related to drug abuse. If an integration between family unity and change occurs, the various family members can grow, develop, and form their new families. If this integration does not occur, the family faces stagnation—difficulties and problems later on.

It is important to understand the stages of family life because this developmental perspective can help one to identify the most problematic stages of the family. For example, many drug problems are linked to the family-life stages of "graduation" from the family and "mourning" important losses. By identifying the life stage of a family it may be possible to clarify the kinds of problems being faced and to develop a preventive program. If there has been a poor resolution of the crisis at any one particular stage, things are bound to be more difficult at the next stage, and the family may have to work on resolving two very different crises at the same time.

STAGES OF FAMILY LIFE

Where to begin on the spiral of family development is arbitrary. There is no clear beginning and no end to a family's development. However, we have chosen the point when two people come together to form a new family: marriage and coupling.

STAGE 1: MARRIAGE AND COUPLING

I believe that getting married to John marked something of significance in my life. But I am not any different than I was the day before I got married. In terms of my drug use and overall personality, nothing has changed.

. . . It's like I'm supposed to be perfect now that John and I are married. The way I am reacting, I try to sabotage the situation . . . I've been going out and buying cocaine with our house money.

These are the words of a recently married woman with a major drug problem. Her difficulty with commitment to the marriage versus commitment to using drugs is not atypical of marriages in which one spouse is a drug abuser.

When couples come together, they need to move toward each other and away from the family of origin. Commitment to forming a new family and to the couple relationship is central to this stage of development. Often the problem of balancing the commitment between the family of origin and the new couple is expressed as a loyalty conflict. In-laws may be pitted against the new couple, or one spouse may accuse the other of "not cutting the apron strings." Also, the new couple needs to clarify their new role as a marital unit. It is essential to work out the ground rules as to who cooks, who cleans, and how money will be spent. Marital dissatisfaction is likely to arise if one spouse is burdened with too much responsibility.

Both the severity of loyalty conflicts and the couples' ability to clarify their new roles will affect the kinds of problems new couples are likely to face at this stage.

When my son and his wife have problems, usually about drugs, he always comes back to me. I've been strong for him: I've had to be his backbone. When he is in a crisis, I'm the one he falls back on. But I'm afraid he will become a child, and I'll have to raise him again.

When one or both spouses resort to drugs, the difficulties are compounded. Whether or not drugs are involved, a common problem at this stage is for one spouse to remain overconnected to a member of the family of origin. In the case cited above, the son has remained in a conflictual and overinvolved relationship with his mother. During times of tension, both may team up against the spouse—who is seen as an outsider. This pattern of relatedness is described as *triangular.* Mother and son are united against the daughter-in-law, who may be viewed as a corrupting influence or simply the "bad one" and used as a scapegoat.

Because the basic issues of commitment to the family of origin and to the new relationship are unresolved, the loyalty triangle may shift from time to time. In an attempt to commit himself to his spouse, the son may unite with his wife against his mother. The mother-in-law now becomes the bad one and serves as a rallying point for the couple. One extreme form of this type of problem is for the couple to reject the family of origin completely. Some couples may move across the country in the false hope of gaining "independence" and cutting the apron strings.

We don't have any family. To all intents and purposes, our families are dead. They are burned out on us and we on them. There is no way they can help either one of us. In any event, my parents are in Indiana. They really don't want to be bothered with us.

When both members of the couple are abusers, drugs can be the point of unity from which to reject the family of origin. The couple intends to gain autonomy by rejecting their family background. Clearly, an independence based on drugs is a false sort of autonomy and one that often leads to a suffocating and destructive closeness for couples.

My family didn't know that I was supporting his habit with my salary. I really can't turn to my family for help because I don't want them to know about our business. I have always thought of addicts as sleazy. I would be terribly ashamed if my family found out.

Drug abuse may alienate and distance this couple from important family resources. Such distancing places undue strain on the young couple, as their relationship is expected to satisfy all their individual needs and compensate for the disconnection from the family of origin. Another example of rejecting the family of origin is when one of the spouses is "adopted" by the family of the other spouse. The extreme form of the loyalty triangle discussed above is for the "outcast" to be taken in by his or her in-laws while renouncing the family of origin. Eventually, the adopted family serves as a staging ground where the "adopted" member recreates the conflicts and patterns of the family of origin.

STAGE 2: PARENTHOOD

With the birth of the first child a permanent transformation takes place—parenthood. Spouses can reverse a marital relationship through divorce or separation, but parenthood is irreversible. The parent will always be the child's biological father or mother, no matter who raises the child. This second stage of family life refers to the changes that occur with the birth of the first child and the subsequent tasks of child rearing. The couple must balance marital with parental responsibilities. The central conflict during this stage is balancing the interests of children in relation to the interests of the spouse.

The transformation to parenthood is traditionally marked by social and religious ceremonies. Celebrating the gift of life is common to all cultures, and most religions mark the event with formal rituals such as baptism. However, as we have adapted to the demands of our highly mobile and technological culture, the family has become increasingly nuclear and extended family resources are diminished. Today the responsibility for child rearing is the exclusive domain of parents, whereas fifty to sixty years ago the expectation was that the extended family—grandparents, aunts, uncles —would share in the task. Having less family available for child rearing often overloads young couples who may be struggling with economic survival.

When a couple has children each member's role expands from that of husband or wife to being a parent with responsibility for the life of another. A young child needs care—an infant is completely helpless. The child depends on parents for food, and the parents have to clean up when the baby makes a mess. The parents have to become responsible whether they like it or not. They have a whole set of new pressures and tasks that must be done for this helpless infant. A conflict may arise between the interest of the marital relationship and the interest of the child. The issue becomes who comes first—the parent or the child?

You have to understand that I cannot fully concentrate on you when I am with the baby. The baby doesn't make me irritable. I am her mother. But you and I need to do things together!

If these conflicts of interest are not balanced well, then problems will emerge later on. One problem is a neglect of the marital relationship in favor of full-time parenting. One spouse forgets about the other and the marriage turns into an emotional divorce, even if the couple stays together. One or both parents may dedicate themselves heart and soul to child rearing. This sets the stage for one person, usually the mother, to become overly involved with the child and forget about marital responsibilities. Frequently, the other spouse retreats from the relationship, sometimes to alcohol or drugs.

Well, somebody had to be the "responsible" one. I had a daughter to care for and who needed to be taken care of. He only cared about his drugs and his friends. I don't know how I've put up with this nonsense as long as I have. It's been three years. I don't have much of a husband, but I have my daughter.

Another kind of problem that may emerge at this stage is the neglect or even rejection of the children in favor of the marital relationship. Particularly in drug-abusing families, the typical conflict of "who comes first" (the newborn or the spouse) is translated into the couple choosing between drugs and the child. Too often, drug use will be chosen over the welfare of the children.

We were very involved with each other and with the dope. We only cared about our next fix and took the food and rent money to buy our drugs. Our child was taken away because sometimes she went without food.

Another problem that comes up at this stage is the child caring for the parent through some kind of problematic behavior. A common problem comes at a time when the child is around five or six years of age. The child might develop a sleep disturbance, tantrums, seemingly "uncontrollable" behavior, yell and scream to such a degree that it provokes parental intervention. If the problem is a sleep disturbance, the child might awaken in the middle of the night with terrible nightmares. Mother and father are both awakened, but it is the mother who will most likely stay with the child. If this behavior continues, it may develop into a problem of overinvolvement between the mother and child. If the problem is "uncontrollable" behavior, both parents might have to join forces to deal effectively with their child.

Often what is behind these so called "child" problems is the child's terrible worry about parents fighting too much, that parents may separate, or that one parent might become depressed. The parents may have cared for the child for six years or so, but children have ways of caring for their parents too. Most often, this is out of the realm of awareness of both parents and children. Nevertheless, by becoming a problem the child can bring parents together, at least temporarily. Also, most children are acutely sensitive to the moods and feelings of the adults surrounding them. In some families the child who makes trouble not only keeps both parents busy and together but, most important, may keep one parent from experiencing depression.

STAGE 3: CHILDREN GROWING UP

Children develop increasingly separate identities between the ages of seven and eighteen. The development of a separate identity begins much earlier (for example, when the child is about two he or she learns how to say "no"). However, for the family this stage begins about the time when the firstborn goes to school and continues through the adolescence of the last child. During this time the family members gradually become more independent. The stage of children growing up brings forth a change for parents— from having been used to taking care of their children completely to letting go of them gradually. It is difficult to begin to let go.

Starting school can signal difficulties in letting go. The child might develop a problem when he or she first begins school. The child might have tantrums, yell and scream, and not be able to handle being in school. The child has to be brought back home, and there is no way that the parents can make the child go to school. The end result is that the child stays home. This may be called a "school phobia."

Often what is behind the school phobia is the child's terrible worry about the mother. The child fears that if he or she is not there, mother might become depressed. In a sense the mother needs the child to be home to take care of her, and for her to take care of him. If the mother has been accustomed to taking care of her child for six or seven years and was too involved with the youngster, this overinvolvement is hard to give up. In essence the child going to school means that the mother becomes unemployed. She loses her job at least from 8 A.M. to 3 P.M. This is very difficult, particularly when there are marital problems or when the support that ought to be coming from her husband or parents is not available.

Religious ceremonies such as bar mitzvah and confirmation serve to acknowledge the fact that children are moving out of childhood and into adulthood and thus need a greater degree of independence. Social ceremonies such as "sweet sixteen" birthday parties also provide some social recognition that the children are indeed growing up and becoming adults.

It is during this third stage of family development that drug problems most frequently occur. Problems are likely to emerge if the children are unable to let go of the parents, or if the parents are unable to let go of the children, providing gradually more experiences with separation and autonomy.

My mother is too close to my brother, and he needs to learn to be more on his own. He is forty years old and has never left home. He's never been married. If my mother dies I don't know what would become of him.

When the parents and one child cannot separate because of their overinvolved and intense relationship, the child—now a young adult—remains at home, developing a problem that requires the attention of the parents. If the parents are having difficulties in their marriage, needing to attend to the problems of the young adult serves to rescue them and force them to work together. If during the prior stage mother or father were totally devoted to the child and the marriage relationship weakened, then it would be increasingly difficult for the young adult to let go of the parents and vice versa.

Stubbornness, rebelliousness, or seeming selfishness are characteristic problems in adolescence. These kinds of problems often reflect difficulties on the part of the parents to set consistent terms for household and family rules. Parents are unable to hold the children accountable for their actions. It is not clear who is in charge of the family. If parents and children stay bound up and overly close with one another, this limits the freedom of family members to venture out into the world and to eventually graduate from the family. For the teenager, drugs can be a way to rebel.

I still worry, "Am I going to lose my baby?" My son is thirty-seven years old, married, and with a six-year-old daughter. They live at home with me, but he can't talk to me about drugs . . .

Drugs can sometimes function as a way to resolve the conflict of separation and growing up. First, drug use provides a false sense of individuality. The young adult develops a sense of independence from acquaintances in the drug world. Second, the drug user experiences "individuality" by having drug experiences, which are generally separate from the family. In addition, the person is likely to have setbacks, crises, and difficulties that will provoke parental involvement and thus reinforce the overdependence between parents and young adult.

STAGE 4: CHILDREN LEAVING HOME

The fourth stage entails the actual departure of the children from home. Just as there is a graduation from school, young adults also need to "graduate" from home. The task of the young adult is to move toward a more independent life. As parents let go of the adult children, their task is to begin facing each other and finding another focus for life other than child rearing.

By the time a child finishes adolescence the parents have been in a parenting role for nearly twenty years and have become accustomed to taking care of children. It is not so easy to give up the role of parental caretaker. It is as if they had been told to work on a project for eighteen years, then are suddenly told to forget about it. The parents are left in a vacuum.

Now the parents need to look at one another more and more, examining their relationship as a twosome. What are they going to do now? This dilemma for the parents has been called the "empty nest syndrome." This is another of those critical life events in which the family goes through a dual loss. There is the loss of the children, in terms of their attachment to the parents; and the loss of the parents, in terms of the children who have been attached to them. Both parents and children must find a new focus for their lives.

The crisis is exacerbated in today's culture, where new couples frequently delay having children. In years past the norm was for a young adult to leave the family of origin, marry, and begin having children. This process gave a role to the newly married couple (becoming parents) and also to the couple's parents (becoming grandparents). However, our culture has experienced a change in these norms in recent years. Parenting is delayed, and so is grandparenting. For young couples this change in cultural norms leaves a vacuum that may be filled by paying more attention to each other, or to the careers of one or both spouses, or sometimes by continued postadolescent abuse of drugs. For the parents of the young couple, the vacuum must also be filled.

One problem that comes up at this stage is too much involvement on the part of a parent who does not allow this separation from home. Another is an expulsion of the children from the family. Expelling troubled young adults from home usually results in their failure and eventual return to home. This is the case of children who become runaways—they leave home, go to San Francisco or New York, and get into difficult situations that frequently involve drug abuse.

STAGE 5: INTEGRATION OF LOSS

When I came from Argentina, my husband and I lost contact with our family back home. He later left me. My children and grandchildren have grown up in Texas, as if my family were dead.

Concern with loss, death, or separation is a frequent theme for families with a drug-abusing member. As parents grow older families must face the reality of the aging process and their parents' eventual death. The task for the older couple is to adjust to the new social, economic, and physical loss that comes along with aging. The children need to assume responsibility for the care of their parents. The task for the adult children is to begin repaying parents for what the parents gave them over their growing-up years.

An important task at this stage is mourning losses. This is particularly relevant for families in which one member uses drugs. Sandra Coleman[5] points out that the issues of mourning and loss are often central in families with a drug-abusing member. Unresolved grief or mourning of relationships may be connected to overly intense relationships with children. In this way the death of an intensely loved parent may be particularly difficult for a drug abuser. Likewise, when a mother loses one of her parents, she may pour her energy into caring for one of her children, making separation from the home more difficult.

When my mother died, about fifteen years ago . . . I never really recovered from that. Then my sister died and I went off the deep end. I became more and more devoted to my daughter. I don't think I've been closer to anyone else. Nobody is able to understand her the way I do. I want to do everything possible to help her stop using drugs and become independent.

The loss can be linked to any number of events—migration from another country, divorce, the death of an important family member. A loss that has not been properly mourned can mean problems later on. Some examples: (1) a young man who completely denied the death of his grandparents had tremendous difficulty reinvesting himself in a new relationship to create his own family; (2) an older couple had major unsettled emotional issues with the wife's family of origin. She attempted to pay her deceased parents back for their neglect through an exaggerated dedication to her own children. However, this over-devotion let her children know that she could not tolerate losses or even allow separation. So the family members were trapped in a family system where the over-protection of each other from the pain of loss, death, and separation are the basic rules. Drug abuse often allows one or several family members to escape this overprotection and serves as a means of maintaining a powerful devotion to the family, albeit destructively.

I always thought of myself as an orphan. My parents died when I was young, and my one aunt died in an accident when I was in my teens. My only family has been my daughter, and she is an alcoholic.

This older mother described her family of origin during one of our Community Network educational sessions. It was clear she had suffered many painful and devastating losses. The extent of the losses and her difficulty in mourning are understandable, given her limited resources and age. In a way it is to her credit that she was able to survive essentially alone in the world. However, the problems in mourning the losses may have contributed to a problematic relationship with her daughter, who developed a severe addiction to alcohol.

When we moved to the States, it was as if our family back home had died. I've never gone back to Italy or contacted my family back home.

Migration can be traumatic. One loses not only family, but culture and country as well. Culture shock, adaptation to the new environment, and economic survival all converge to make the process of moving more problematic for the family. Drug abuse, by refocusing attention, can be a way to postpone the mourning of important losses for the family.

VARIATIONS ON THE STAGES OF FAMILY LIFE

For reasons of clarity, a number of variations on the life stages of families were not included in Table 1. We may consider coupling, parenting, growing up, departure of the children, and integration of loss as five major stages in the spiral of family development, but this sequence is often interrupted with divorce, separation, abandonment, or deaths. When remarriage occurs, a blended family is formed. The issues to be considered for single-parent and blended families are somewhat different, as they are for childless couples and couples with adopted children. At a minimum, a more complete framework of family development must include single-parent families and blended or reconstituted families, because they present special issues as related to drug abuse.

SINGLE-PARENT FAMILIES

Throughout history when men left the home, either in the pursuit of war or peace, it was the women who raised the children. Single-parent families are not new; what is new is that we now refer to these families with new-found respect and dignity. Instead of using such negative terms as "broken homes" or "unwed mothers," our society has begun to recognize the dignity of a parent alone, rearing children. A single-parent family can occur at any point in the life cycle, as soon as reproductive maturity is reached. With separation, divorce, or teenage pregnancy, often it is the mother who becomes the head of household and carries the burden for raising the children. Indeed, as the divorce rate escalates, single-parent families are becoming increasingly the norm in the United States.

It's an awful big burden for one person to work and raise a large family. My son started using drugs about the time my husband and I were having problems. My husband left, and we have not heard from him since. I had to be both a father and mother to my five children.

These are the words of a woman who, in her mid-thirties, became the head of a single-parent family. The burdens on her and her children were extremely difficult, as she was the primary provider of food, clothing, shelter, discipline, and love.

The tasks for a single-parent family are more complex at the different stages of the family life span. When father and mother split up, a central task for the families is to ensure that children can still have adequate access to both parents. If the children become a battleground for postmarital tensions, then they will be placed in the impossible position of rescuing the adults and/or having to choose between the parents. Ivan Boszormenyi-Nagy[6] writes of *split-loyalty* conflicts to represent the kind of bind that children are in when the expression of affection to one parent is considered as disloyalty by another. The children are confused and resentful about being in this position, and drug abuse can be one way for them to rebel.

If only one parent is available, a task for the family will be to establish a network of adults that can serve as support for the parent and the children. The problems of parental-child overinvolvement described earlier may become magnified. To some extent overinvolvement is unavoidable, because the social reality of single-parent families is one of isolation with limited resources for psychological nourishment and affection. As isolation pulls for overdependence and overinvolvement, it may be more difficult for children to separate from the family at later stages.

Alternatively, the single parent may view the children as burdensome, restricting the parent's possibilities in developing adult relationships, as well as career opportunities. Parent and children may turn against one another. Children may find themselves as the target of parental anger, frustration, and disappointment. This often leads to escaping the impossible situation through running away, antisocial activity, or drug abuse. As we discuss in a later chapter, one key to avoiding these problems is to build ties with the extended family, increasing the economic and emotional resources for both the children and the single parent.

BLENDED OR RECONSTITUTED FAMILIES

We were at the recital where my daughter from my first marriage was giving her first performance. I was there with her stepfather—my husband. My ex-husband and his family had come too. If this weren't enough, we were all seated in the same row. When the recital was over, I was terribly worried about how my daughter was going to handle this situation with her friends. How would she introduce her father? How would she introduce her stepfather, even her stepmother? Well, she came over and without even thinking said to her best friend: "This is my Mommy and Daddy from Idaho and this is my Mommy and Daddy from Montana."

This account captures the successful resolution of a split-loyalty conflict. Blended families—parents with children from former marriages who remarry—are a special case. A framework of family life stages needs to recognize those families that experience a divorce. The family might move through a stage of living as single-parent families for a while, then with a remarriage they form another stage consisting of a blended family with stepparents.

The advantage of step and blended families is that they provide additional human and economic resources. In this sense, the step or blended family may be in a better position to handle the tasks, conflicts, and problems of the expanding and contracting family stages.

However, the disadvantage is the careful balancing required of parents to settle their conflicts without involving the children—

even after divorce. The potential for split loyalty conflicts is great; this can be minimized by insuring that the children can have reasonable access to both sets of parents.

I know it's not fair for them to be in the middle, but what can you do? When their father is late with the support money they go without their allowance. I just can't make ends meet, and it's not fair either to have their stepfather be doing what their father should be doing! So the children are constantly watching for the mail to see if the check arrived. When they ask about their allowance I tell them their father hasn't sent the support money yet.

It was probably not a coincidence that the middle daughter of this family expressed her rebellion through drug abuse, perhaps as a way to provoke her father's intervention in these unsettled family issues. An important task for blended families is to work as a team of adults taking into consideration the welfare interests of their children. Often with the problems of drugs there will be an ongoing questioning of parental authority, particularly the authority of the stepparent. Parents need to work as a team, despite continual challenges to their authority.

One family at one of our Community Network meetings explained how they handled the problem:

Father: *We are together on how to work as a team. She is a stepmother, but a very good stepmother.*

Stepmother: *I don't tell him anything. All I do is listen. Sometimes, I give him my thoughts. Sometimes he doesn't like it, but that's it. We work as a team on this. That's why I'm here.*

Each phase of family development has typical problems, a specific conflict, and tasks that have to be mastered. The framework of stages of family life provides a way of understanding what some of the issues are, and problems that families face as they develop. Crises occur at every stage, for every family. The key is for families to resolve the crisis at each stage. This chapter points out ways that drug abuse can be involved in each stage of family development. At each stage, drug abuse can reflect the struggles of a particular individual in the family life cycle. Understanding the stages of family life can help a family to predict where problems are likely to occur, and to help the drug abuser understand the emotional basis of his or her substance abuse. The way in which these themes are handed down from generation to generation is the subject of the next chapter.

4. Family Patterns Across Generations

And visit the sins of the fathers upon the children unto the third and fourth generation.

Ecclesiastes 1:8

I don't want my children to have to go through what I had to go through. I want a better life for my children.

The notion that families pass on to future generations their culture, traditions, beliefs, and identity, as well as their sins, has been with us at least since the writing of the Old Testament. However old the idea might be, there has been a great deal of interest among mental health professionals in studying and understanding how certain traditions or patterns of behavior are transmitted from one generation to the next. Family-oriented clinicians have noted that while most parents will want a better life for their children, many will—consciously or unconsciously—repeat with their children what was done to them.

The roots of drug abuse can often be traced to two, three, or more generations in the history of a family. The historical context of families with a drug-abusing member often reveals legacies of alcohol abuse, death, traumatic separations, migration, and loss. Learning about our family history can go a long way in teaching us about ourselves, our loved ones, and how we can initiate change. If we ignore our family history, we may unwittingly repeat family errors that grow in magnitude with each successive generation.

HOW TO MAKE A FAMILY TREE

I have a much more clear idea of who my parents are and the problems they faced after doing my family tree . . . I was able to see them as human beings trying to do the best they could. . . . Now, maybe I can forgive them.

I didn't think I would learn anything from the family tree business because I feel I know my family better than anybody. Now, I can see how I probably contributed to my son's problems. It's no coincidence that the same thing happened between my parents and me.

I always thought that my husband is the one with the drug problem. The family tree showed me that I have been doing the same thing his mother did for ages. I'm the responsible one and the caretaker. He's the irresponsible one who needs someone to care for him.

These are the comments of a brother, a mother, and a wife of an addict. All were asked do do their family trees and were helped in searching for patterns during one of our Community Network training programs.

Family trees or *genograms* are diagrams of the family that include not only the current generation but also two or three generations —parents, grandparents, and perhaps great-grandparents. These family diagrams are of interest because they can help identify untapped resources in the family system. Family trees can also help people identify and understand where certain patterns come from. In most families patterns are passed on from one generation to the next. Some values, ideals, and expectations may be constructive and desirable. Others may be destructive. The idea is to identify these patterns and learn how to put an end to the maladaptive ones that may be linked to destructive behaviors such as drug abuse.

The use of genograms was pioneered by Murray Bowen[1] as part of his intergenerational family systems theory. Genograms are now used by a variety of mental health professionals working with a wide range of problems. Bowen and his colleagues, notably Monica McGoldrick[2], developed a set of symbols that have become standard in the field, and which we will use throughout this chapter (see footnote to Figure 1).

For example, squares are used to represent males and circles for females. Horizontal lines connect people of the same generation, and vertical lines connect parent-child relationships. Deceased members are represented by an X drawn within the circle or square. Marriages are illustrated by a vertical line below the circle and one below the square, and then connected by a horizontal line. Children are listed in birth order beginning on the left with the oldest child.

Following are the instructions[3] distributed to families we work with on a regular basis. Family members are given these instructions with the task of making a first attempt at a family tree. We use the family tree[4] with families in the Community Network project and with families in the Intergenerational Family Therapy project.

INSTRUCTIONS FOR COMPLETING YOUR FAMILY TREE*

A genogram is a chart showing the relationship of all members of a given family. Making a genogram helps (a) to understand the significance of these relationships and (b) to plan about things that can be done to improve family relationships.

Key symbols are
☐ square for males
○ circle for females

For each family member include (wherever possible):

1. Name
2. Age
3. Date of birth: day, month, year
4. Date of marriages
5. Date of separations
6. Date of divorces
7. Date of death (for children include miscarriages and still-births)
8. Important life events (and dates) that have had a major impact on your life or on the lives of your relatives

---

*These instructions were adapted from work by Bowen (1980) and are used with permission.

9. Occupation
10. Illness: include information about chronic physical disease or chronic emotional disorders
11. Place of residence

Steps to complete the genogram or family tree:

1. Start with yourself as a point of reference.
2. Then list your spouse and children, brothers and sisters (and persons to whom your brothers and sisters are married).
3. Then move back a generation and provide the same information about your parents, their siblings, spouses and children.
4. Sometimes the requested information is difficult to find; try to get as much information as you can. The more information you have the easier it will be to identify unrecognized factors that are feeding into the problem you are currently having.

HOW TO BEGIN A FAMILY TREE

Let us begin by drawing the family tree of Carlos, a colleague of the authors (see Figure 1). Carlos is thirty-four and Maria is thirty-two. They were married in 1983.

Note that the square represents a male, Carlos, and the circle represents a female, Maria. As Carlos is the central focus of this genogram, a double square is drawn around him. Write the ages of the various people inside the circles or squares, or enter dates of births. The horizontal line that connects Carlos and Maria shows that they are married. Write the date of marriage right on the horizontal line.

The children of this couple are illustrated by drawing two vertical lines from the marriage (horizontal) line. This shows that their firstborn is now a three-year-old daughter and their second born is now a two-year-old son. If Carlos and Maria had any adopted children, this would be designated by a dotted vertical line.

So far, we have drawn the nuclear family structure, that is, the

Figure 1

How to Begin a Family Tree*

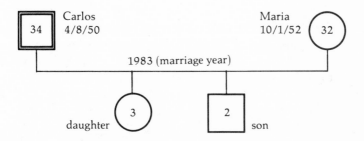

Key to symbols used in family trees:

☐ = male		⎮ = children
○ = female		⋮ = adopted children
☐ = male central focus		= overinvolved relationship
○ = female central focus		= distant relationship
⊠ = deceased male		= conflictual relationship
⊗ = deceased female		= cutoff/stagnant relationship
— = marriage		

parents and their children. The family tree can be expanded to include the family of origin. We will draw Carlos's side of the family first. Figure 2 shows that he is the second born in a family of six.

Carlos's father is sixty-five and his mother is sixty. Reading from left to right, we see that the oldest brother is thirty-nine years old. He is married and has three children. Carlos is the second born. The third born is a thirty-year-old brother who is married and has no children. The youngest sibling is a twenty-five year-old married female with a one-year-old boy.

In developing the family tree it is useful to make all kinds of notations along the way. Write down where people live, what work they do, and other special or interesting things. In Carlos's case, his parents live in New Jersey. The older brother moved back to New Jersey after living in Mexico for five years. The third born has moved around the country a lot. He has lived in Illinois, South Carolina, Arizona, Florida, and is currently in Texas.

At this point we could expand Carlos's family tree in several directions. We could develop his father's side or his mother's side of the family. We could gather information about Maria's family of origin. It is generally helpful to have a lot of paper available to keep track of the different lines in the family genealogy.

INTERPRETING THE FAMILY TREE

Much can be deduced from the information we have on Carlos's family. First, the family of origin is at a specific *life stage* where parents are relatively alone and have to face one another after the children have grown up. Carlos and Maria, as a family, are at an early stage of parenthood. One question would be how the family has handled these two simultaneously occurring stages. In Chapter 3 we discussed the stages of *parenthood* and *integration of loss*. A complicating factor for the family may be that they are spread rather far apart from each other. Carlos and Maria are in Los Angeles, as is the younger sister, while the parents are in New Jersey. The parents actually have an "empty nest," and the older

Figure 2

Example of a Family Tree

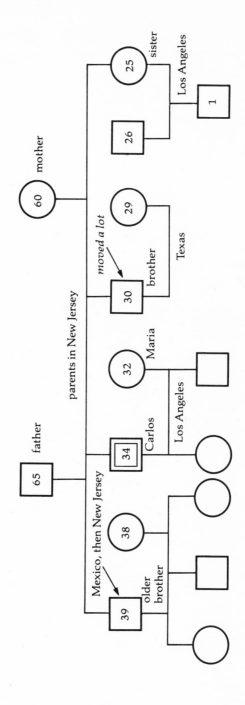

brother has only recently returned to New Jersey. The parents' situation might be eased if they could act as grandparents. However, Carlos and Maria are far away geographically. The older brother could serve as a resource for the parents if they got along; the problem is that they do not. There has been a long dispute between the older brother, his parents, and his wife; this is a common conflictual pattern which we call *loyalty triangles.* These conflicts can be diagrammed as triangles, and they are something to look for in family trees, since they can be a source of stress and tension.

Carlos has been an important focus for the family for some time. He has had the role of being eccentric, strange, oppositional, and at times the black sheep. He was at one corner of the triangle, with mother and father at the other two corners. Through him, the family joined together. His parents appeared to present a united front in the face of Carlos's problematic behavior. Otherwise, the parents might be arguing and fighting among themselves. Fortunately, in his family, the position of center of attention was well shared: It was passed down from one sibling to the next. A more problematic picture emerges when one member is stuck in this role. When Carlos moved out of the role of being "special," he was replaced by the younger sibling. Then the youngest sister took on the task of being the black sheep. The parents were kept rather busy as they tended to the problems presented by their children.

One of the important issues for this family was their migration from Chile to the United States. This meant a major crisis and a disruption of ties with family, country, and culture. It was also a loss of status for the family in general, and for Carlos's father in particular. Thus the family faced the normal pressures and conflicts at this stage of the life cycle, as well as facing the tensions and pressures created by their migration to the United States.

When he constructed his family tree Carlos discovered how much he knew about his mother's side of the family and how little he knew about his father's side. Carlos's family left Chile shortly after the fall of the democratic government in 1973. Thus there were many *cutoffs* or stagnant relationships with his father's side of the family due to the migration, the distance, and political differences. Stagnation of a relationship occurs when loyalty is disrupted (for example, when relatives break contact with each other) and trust erodes. This realization led him to reestablish contact with *unused resources*—relatives on his father's side of the family— as a means of establishing trust in relationships. However, reconnecting meant returning to Chile, where there was still a difficult political situation.

Nevertheless, Carlos reconnected with aunts, uncles, and cousins by visiting his family's homeland. He was welcomed into the family after a twelve-year absence and felt at home with them. Carlos was able to learn a tremendous amount about his family and about Chile, and to establish personal relationships with extended family members. Where there had been cutoffs and disconnections, renewed relationships emerged. However, his trip to Chile forced him to take a firm stance in relation to his parents, who opposed the visit. Essentially, they feared for his life, since several family members had "disappeared." Although somewhat dangerous, the trip was symbolic of action based on convictions that may go against the wishes of other family members. Carlos needed to see things for himself, reconnect with family, and travel to Chile. As adults, he and his parents could disagree without their disagreement signaling a betrayal or a threat to the relationship. Developing adult relationships with one's parents is a theme we will return to with a number of families.

How roles are passed on from one generation to the next is something else to look for in doing family trees. We call this process the *revolving slate*[5] or the *generational transmission process.* When Carlos studied his family in depth, one of his important discoveries was the similarity between him and an uncle who had remained in Chile, and with whom he had been compared when he was a child. The uncle was in a role similar to the one Carlos held in the current generation of his family—namely, the person viewed as eccentric, difficult, the one with strong ideas. Also, both were lawyers. The connection Carlos made between what had happened in the prior generation and with the current one served to help him view his family as a *human* or *emotional system* with a life of its own. Carlos had always believed himself to be acting from his own set of principles and ideals. When he examined his family tree, however, he discovered an important precedent in the family for this behavior. It was as if a script had been written, at least one generation before, which he was following to the letter. Thus his seeming eccentric and oppositional role was one way of showing *invisible loyalty* to the family of origin by keeping certain traditions and actions alive in the current generation. In some families a drug-abuse problem may be passed down through the same process of intergenerational transmission. Father may have had a problem with alcohol. Following in his father's footsteps, the son may develop a problem with drugs.

Making a family tree helped Carlos see his family in a larger perspective, taking into consideration a variety of contexts. Later the issue became how he could *serve as a resource* by focusing less on changing others and more on how to *improve relationships* in the family. Carlos opted for trying to develop one-to-one relationships with each member of his family, as a means of avoiding triangulations and developing more personal and adult relationships. Based on his understanding of the family tree, Carlos renewed relationships with both parents and siblings.

When one works on a family tree it is helpful to think about areas of conflict, the potential effect of losses, and the roles different family members have held. Who has been the responsible one? Who has been the irresponsible one? What are the stories of success and failure? What are the areas of strength and what are the weaknesses? Who has been "disowned" by the family? Who has had a drinking problem? Who has been depressed? These kinds of questions may help family members to arrive at a more complete and complex picture of the family.

However, while these patterns may have their roots in the prior generations, the family is not to blame for these patterns. More often than not, the family's subjective reality is conditioned by larger and more powerful forces—the economic, social, and political context in which the family is embedded. From our perspective the family is not the victimizer, but rather the victim. The goal in doing family trees is to understand limiting and unhelpful family patterns so that resources can be identified and strategies for change can be worked on.

INTERGENERATIONAL PATTERNS AND DRUG ABUSE

In this section we will examine the generational patterns of several families with major drug abuse problems. While there are no distinct patterns that apply to all families with a drug-abusing member, this section should serve as a guide to concepts and principles that may help in identifying patterns—that is, repetitive sequences of behavior that may be connected to drug abuse.

Most of the research with families that have a member with a drug abuse problem suggests that these families have a great deal of difficulty with "closeness," perhaps too much closeness or over-involvement with the drug-abusing child or young adult.[6] If the abuser is an adolescent, drug use can serve as a way to express rebelliousness in attempts to separate from the family of origin. If the problem is specific to the life cycle stage of children growing up, then the adolescent may simply grow out of the drug abuse, or the family may find a way to adjust to the call for greater autonomy. However, if the drug problem is more deep-seated, it is likely to involve intergenerational conflicts of closeness and separation. Indeed, the families of addicts have been found to differ from other problemed families in terms of the high prevalence of intergenerational chemical dependence, direct and open expression of conflicts, strong family bonds, and a preoccupation with themes of death, loss, and separation.[7]

SEARCHING FOR PATTERNS

One goal of identifying intergenerational patterns is to better understand how the family has responded to stressful events in the past. Such understanding can lead to corrective and preventive action. The pioneer theoretical writings of Ivan Boszormenyi-Nagy[8] are particularly useful in understanding intergenerational relationships. We have drawn from his theory of relationships four basic concepts that can be useful in finding intergenerational patterns: (1) loyalty triangles; (2) the revolving slate; (3) stagnant relationships or cutoffs; and (4) the social context.

LOYALTY TRIANGLES

Loyalty is one way to think about the unifying bond of closeness in family relationships. Loyalty triangles can be diagrammed on a family tree to illustrate how three individuals are bonded to each other. Common loyalty triangles occur when a family member is in a position of having to choose between: (1) a parent and a spouse; (2) a spouse and the children; or (3) the parents and the children. For example, a man and his wife may be at two ends of the triangle, with his parents at the other end. The triangular relationship works in the following way: If the man shows loyalty to his wife, this is a betrayal of his parents. If he shows loyalty to his parents, it means a betrayal of his wife. Loyalty may be direct and visible, or indirect and seemingly invisible.[9] One common dynamic of drug abuse is the addict who remains invisibly loyal to the family of origin at great personal cost. Loyalty triangles can also help clarify the delicate balance of burden and benefits in family relationships.

REVOLVING SLATE

The revolving slate describes the intergenerational transmission process. Family traits are passed from generation to generation, as if written on a chalkboard of entered accounts. Once we have identified loyalty triangles, it may be possible to see if these triangles flip-flop from one generation to the next. Thus, while the cast of characters may change, the loyalty triangles remain the same, trapping people in the process.

A common clinical observation of drug-abusing couples is that they reproduce in their marital relationships similar roles and patterns to those they had with the family of origin; this is one example of the revolving slate. Each may be using the other to settle unpaid emotional accounts in the family of origin. Also, in families with a drug-abusing member, there is typically an inter-generational history of drug and alcohol abuse and a legacy of catastrophic losses and premature separations. These are heavy burdens for the current and future generations.

STAGNANT RELATIONSHIPS OR CUTOFFS

The third notion is that of cutoffs or stagnant relationships in the family. Distrust and abuse in close relationships leads to distance and disconnection. The distance need not be geographical, but can also be emotional. Facing the erosion of trust and making moves toward establishing trust-based relationships helps to counter the stagnation and cutoffs.

Trust is a key issue for families with a drug abuse problem. The addict cannot be trusted, but neither can the addict trust the family. Often, the male or female drug abuser has had a history of victimization and self-sacrifice, often to protect the family.

THE CONTEXT

The fourth concept is that of the economic, social, political, and cultural contexts in which the family is embedded. Too often the economic resources of the family limit a healthy development. Understanding the specifics of the environment in which the family is enmeshed can serve to clarify how these family intergenerational patterns have their roots in the broader context.

For example, the mid-1960s to late 1970s was a period marked by a great deal of experimentation with drugs. For some, this time and context was an introduction to the world of drugs. The times were changing as a counterculture was evolving. Drug use was a vehicle of rebellion and many were trapped in a context that supported drug use.

EXAMPLES OF THE FAMILY TREE AND DRUG ABUSE

The Antonio Family Tree

Let's look at the family tree of Eduardo Antonio, Jr., a drug abuser. The Antonio family was originally from the Dominican Republic. The drug abuser's mother migrated to the San Francisco Bay Area in 1951 and was the sixth child in a family of ten. Her younger sister, Alberta, was the first to come to the States and served as a *bridge* or *scout* for the family. This is a common pattern with immigrant families. Often one family member is entrusted with the *mission* or task of scouting new territory. Such people have the important role of serving as the bridge between the country of origin and the new context for the family. Often these family members are in positions of having too much responsibility.

As Figure 3 shows, Mrs. Antonio has been married four times and divorced three times. She had one child from the second marriage, Eduardo Jr., who is married and has two boys and a girl. Mrs. Antonio cared for the baby girl, her granddaughter, born in 1979.

LOYALTY TRIANGLES

Mrs. Antonio described a problematic and tense relationship with her daughter-in-law, Jean. She noted that her son did well when his wife, an addict, was either away or in jail. When his wife was out of jail or back living with Eduardo he would do poorly, start abusing drugs again, and not properly care for his children. This *loyalty triangle* was clearly evident for the current generation. We can diagram loyalty triangles that characterize the relationships between generations of this family. The relationship between Mrs. Antonio, Eduardo Jr., and Jean that existed when Jean was in jail is represented in Figure 4a. There are solid ties between Mrs. Antonio and her son, with distant ties between each of them and Jean. When Jean returned, she and Eduardo attempted to build their own family. Jean and Eduardo solidified their relationship, distancing themselves from Mrs. Antonio. The longstanding over-

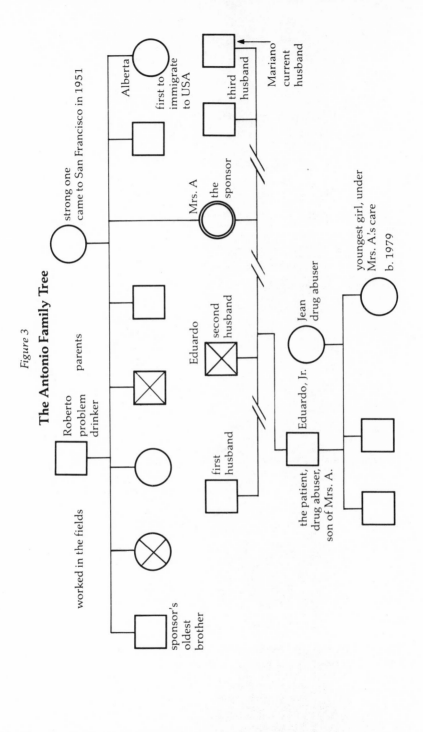

Figure 3

The Antonio Family Tree

Figure 4

Loyalty Triangles of the Antonio Family

A.

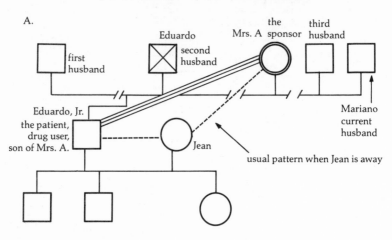

usual pattern when Jean is away

B.

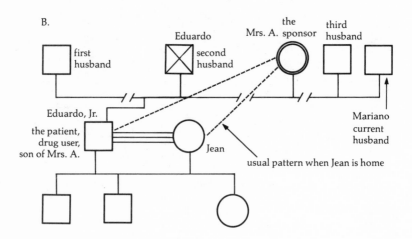

usual pattern when Jean is home

involved relationship between Mrs. Antonio and her son made it difficult to change things. At times, both Eduardo and his mother would team up against his wife. When Jean was around, Eduardo would team up with her against his mother (Figure 4b). Mother became the "bad one," the meddler. A positive connection to Jean would be seen as a threat to mother, and a positive connection to mother would be seen as disloyalty to Jean.

No one was free to show loyalty directly. Indirectly, however, Eduardo's behavior may be interpreted as destructively loyal to his family of origin, in that he remained available to mother as someone to care for. Indeed, drug abuse allowed Eduardo to be both in and out of the family.[10] On the one hand, through the incompetence of drug abuse, he remained as someone to be taken care of by his mother; this supported her in her role of caretaker, at a great cost to Eduardo. On the other hand drug abuse served to get him out of the family, albeit temporarily, through the experience of being high. Drug use also provided him with a false sense of competence in relation to his peers and spouse.

THE REVOLVING SLATE

When Mrs. Antonio delved into her relationships with her parents and husbands using the genogram, a similar pattern of loyalty triangles emerged. Figure 3 illustrates Mrs. Antonio's family of origin relationships. Mrs. Antonio described an overly dependent relationship with mother and a distant one with father, who was a problem drinker. She married four times, and each marital relationship was problematic. Mrs. Antonio has remained available to her mother, and here we see how these loyalty triangles are repeated from generation to generation. A family therapist might ask if the cutoff between Mrs. Antonio and her alcoholic father was being compensated for by overinvolvement with her son. Was she trying to give to her father by overgiving through her son? Was Mrs. Antonio, like her son, trapped in a position where loyalty to her spouse meant disloyalty to her mother?

SOCIAL CONTEXT AND FAMILY RESOURCES

The *strengths* of the Antonio family are evident in its size and the centeredness of the women. As the genogram shows, the family is matriarchal or mother centered. The women are the ones who carry out the family traditions and functions, and the men appear as peripheral or secondary. This structural element may be linked to the family's economic root, which was in sugar farming.

Historically, Caribbean countries have had three basic cash crops. Family structures tend to differ, depending on the nature of the agricultural product with which the family is associated.[11] The Antonio family was connected to the harvest of a crop for which the men were forced to migrate away from home to find work during the "dead time." These families tend to function as single-parent families six months out of the year. The women become the heads of the families by necessity, and the families become more susceptible to disruptions. The family's cohesion suffers. Because of the families' way of making a living, these families become women centered. In contrast, families that work together in the harvest tend to be more cohesive and suffer fewer family disruptions. The Antonio family was an example of such a family that suffered many economic and material hardships with its roots in the social and economic context.

FAMILY CUTOFFS

A third area concerns the cutoffs from family and culture in the Caribbean. While Mrs. Antonio's mother and two sisters were in the San Francisco Bay Area, her father remained in the Caribbean. Also, one of her brothers had died. Loss of country and family depleted her resources and created a situation in which she could only depend on her mother and son, thus setting the stage for overly involved and intense family relationships.

SUMMARY

The Antonio family tree helps to identify loyalty triangles that trap family members in false binds. The Antonios suffered from multiple losses as a result of their migration, reducing their human resources. As we extend our field of vision to both the social and family context, we find that the family is not to blame, nor are its members to blame for the problematic patterns connected to drug abuse. What is important is to identify these patterns, develop an understanding of their roots, and actively work toward improving relationships.

THE BERMAN FAMILY TREE

The Berman family shows a different set of strengths and weaknesses, which are revealed in its genogram. Mrs. Berman's nuclear family consisted of her husband, who died in 1975 of cancer, and her five children. Her husband was a longshoreman, born in the United States and of Polish descent. The three oldest children were daughters. Both boys were addicted to heroin. The older son started abusing drugs at age twenty and has been considered a "bad influence" on the younger son, who started abusing while in his teens.

LOYALTY TRIANGLES

Mrs. Berman had a longstanding problematic relationship with her husband and her sons. She often united with the children against the husband, generally when he was drinking or gambling too much. When the father was around, he would become more involved in the problems with the kids. This was particularly the case when the son's problems with "softer" drugs developed into a major drug problem. At this time, mother and father united against the "problem" children.

Figure 5 shows this configuration. It was almost as if the only thing that kept the family together was the children's drug abuse. When the oldest son successfully completed a treatment program

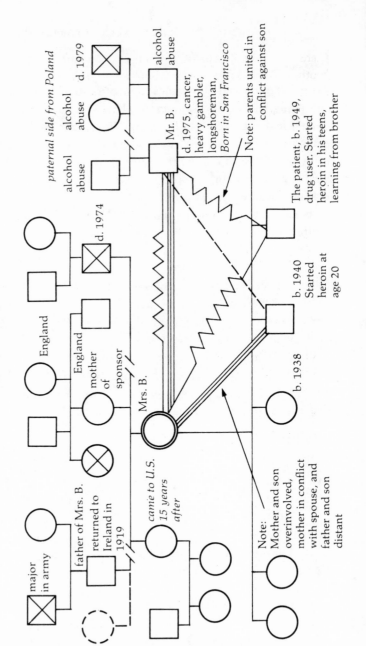

Figure 5

The Berman Family Tree

there was a replacement for him in the family—the younger brother. The loyalty dynamic here might be that the only option for the children in contributing to the family is through a career as a failure through drug abuse. In this way, they avoid facing the painful issues of leaving the parental nest and enable the parents to remain in their role as caretakers.

STAGNANT RELATIONSHIPS AND CUTOFFS

Mrs. Berman was born in the United States of an Irish father and an English mother. Her father returned to Ireland in 1919 and her mother remained in the United States with Mrs. Berman. Mrs. Berman's family of origin experienced a number of severe cutoffs that resulted from the migration to the United States and left the family with few human resources. Mrs. Berman had little access to the paternal side of her family or to her maternal grandparents and maternal aunts. Given these losses, she had done exceedingly well for herself and her children. During one Community Network session, Mrs. Berman discussed the possibility of reconnecting with family in Ireland, England, and California as a means to tap into unused resources.

REVOLVING SLATE

Mr. Berman's family revealed a *legacy* characterized by alcohol abuse and addictive behaviors. His father and mother were described as alcoholics, and Mrs. Berman described her husband as a gambler. In therapy she considered the idea of helping her sons connect with the positive side of their father's legacy. He too had suffered severe disconnection from his country of origin, as his family had migrated from Poland. One possibility was to connect with some aspect of father's history and family of which the sons actually knew little.

SUMMARY

The Berman family illustrates the intergenerational nature of drug abuse. Families with a member addicted to drugs sometimes show legacies of major losses and substance abuse that deplete the familial resources and compound the problem. Clarity about these legacies can be a first step to taking concrete action to stop the intergenerational transmission of drug abuse.

The family is an important and valuable resource. Family members are entitled to learn about their past, examine what has gone on before them, and decide whether or not it is important to develop or renew relationships with other people in the family; this may range from first cousins to distant third and fourth cousins and great-grandparents! The important issue here is to develop relationships directly rather than through a third person. In Chapter 5 we will discuss specific guidelines for how to achieve this goal.

Drug abuse can bring shame, dishonor, recrimination, and blame to the family. The intensity of these feelings serves to further isolate and fragment the family. Examining one's family roots can break the barriers of isolation and perhaps turn feelings of shame into pride, prejudice into acceptance, ignorance into knowledge, and cutoffs into connectedness.

We should note that, while the family patterns discussed in this section tend to be passed on from one generation to the next, there are limitations to this approach. First, no one pattern applies to all families, and there are important ethnic differences.[12] Second, the fact that patterns are transmitted across generations *does not mean that families biologically inherit drug abuse* or that this is a genetic problem. We acknowledge that there is probably a genetic component to susceptibility to substance abuse, but *no one is predestined to be a drug abuser.*

However, much can be done by clarifying the historical family context and understanding loyalty triangles, cutoffs, and the revolving slate. As we have suggested throughout this chapter, learning about one's family history, making an effort to reconnect with family members, and developing trust in relationships can bring about changes by freeing family members from the chain of invisible loyalties transmitted from generation to generation.

II. HOW FAMILIES CHANGE

5. How a Family Perspective Can Help

WHAT IS A FAMILY PERSPECTIVE?

Taking a family perspective means seeing the family as a total system. From this vantage point family patterns can be identified, roles can be detected, and a new vision can be developed. The drug abuse that was previously not well understood as an individually motivated action can be connected to two, three, or more individuals. Through the family looking glass a course of action by one or several family members can often be recognized as having been charted several generations before. At times it seems as if an invisible script written generations before has been unwittingly followed to fulfill an important family legacy.

Using this family perspective can initially make the problem seem more complex and difficult. Trying to figure out how to do things differently presents a challenge to those of us who are used to thinking in individual terms.

THE MEANING OF CHANGE

Change, from a family perspective, means *reflection linked to action* and action based upon reflection. Understanding that the family is a system is a first step toward change. Planning what to do differently based on that understanding is a second step. Implementing the plan is the third step.[1]

When drug abuse afflicts someone in the family, there may be too much action and too little reflection. Family members alternately blame and rescue the troubled person. The family flies from one crisis to the next, with the drug abuser at the center of the turmoil. This leaves little time for thinking out a long-term plan of action. The family may continually respond to emergencies and difficulties that seem only to get worse. Action without reflection is reactive rather than proactive, and sometimes it maintains the patterns of drug abuse.

The Allen family illustrates how reactive family members can unwittingly contribute to the problems of drug abuse. Andrea Allen, thirty-three, lives with her mother, brother, uncle, and nephew. Several family members have rescued her from difficulties with the law, the community, and the home. Typically, the rescue involves money. She often asks for and is given money by several family members. Her mother says,

I know she uses it for drugs, but if I don't give it to her I'm afraid she'll steal it and land in jail again. Then we'd have to bail her out, and things would go from bad to worse . . .

These protective reactions, without an understanding of how they are actually contributing to the drug abuse, serve to maintain the family in a reactive position and trap everyone in a destructive family system.

Reflection without action presents another kind of problem. Guilt, shame, and other emotions can prevent families from taking decisive action based on reflection. Reflection without action may take the form of "I should have done this," or "where did I go wrong with her," leaving a family member feeling stuck and demoralized. Reflection without action is an empty enterprise that only serves to maintain the status quo. During a therapy interview, Mrs. Allen noted,

I just don't know what to do . . . I'm at my wits' end. I blame myself, I guess. I sent her to be raised by her grandmother. I didn't think I could be a good mother, and I guess I was right. Look at her now!

With the help of a therapist, she began to examine what she could realistically give her daughter now. Also, she recognized how she was partly feeding into the drug abuse. A plan was elaborated to help her daughter by saying "no" to her requests for money. If she was able to say "no" to daughter's requests for money, her daughter eventually might be able to say "no" to drugs.

One important step for the Allen family was to recognize how, *as a family,* they were linked together in ways that contributed to the drug abuse. Later, this chapter examines in detail the notion of the family as a system. For the Allen family, the recognition of how each family member encouraged the abuse of drugs by giving Andrea money that she used to buy drugs was a first important step toward change. Family members were able to reflect and examine their actions and reactions without blaming either themselves or others.

Once there is some clarity about the nature of the problem, a course of action can be developed. With the Allens, the plan was to set limits with Andrea by not giving her money. All family members agreed to this strategy, and the plan was to carry out this task for one week, at which point the efforts would be evaluated.

WAYS TO LOOK AT CHANGE

Change affects all family members. How a person looks at change is critical, because the perspective taken to understand change, more often than not, spells out the particular course of action. If one is clear on the perspective taken concerning change, then there is more freedom of movement when things do not seem to change. Another perspective can be adopted and new methods tried.

INDIVIDUAL PERSPECTIVE

If we think of drug abuse exclusively in individual terms, then only the person with the drug problem needs to change. For example, Peter is a thirty-year-old graphic artist with a severe addiction to drugs. His problem may be thought of as some kind of character defect. He might have a weak will, poor self-control, or an internal *psychological* conflict that compels him to abuse drugs. We can think of Peter as having a *biological* problem or some kind of disease with his neurological makeup that leads him to abuse drugs. Peter's problem can also be regarded as a *moral* one—that Peter is just plain bad, a corrupt individual, or a sinner.

From an individual perspective, solutions to the problem are limited to the individual. The solution requires some change inside the person. Peter then needs to resolve his internal conflicts, learn new behaviors and habits, take medication for his disease, or seek salvation in some kind of religious healing. When these approaches have been tried without success, it may be worthwhile to consider another perspective.

TRANSACTIONAL PERSPECTIVE

We can think of the drug problem as involving two people, for example, a troublesome couple relationship with disturbed interactions between a drug abuser and his wife. From this transactional view, addiction is a symptom of other disturbed interactions. The relationship needs to be treated, and patterns of interaction must change to deal effectively with the drug abuse.

A transactional perspective complicates Peter's situation by extending the problem to include his wife of ten years, Janet. From this perspective, neither Janet nor Peter are individually to blame for the drug problem. However, together as a couple and through their interactions they maintain the problem. It is as if their *relationship* were the problem. To change, both would need to relate in a different way.

INTERGENERATIONAL PERSPECTIVE

A third way to look at change goes beyond the individual or the couple, to the family of origin. More people are involved and connected to the problem. Drug abuse is seen as tied to the family tree—a symptom of disturbed intergenerational family relationships. The drug abuser may serve a number of important functions for the family, though at great personal and family cost. From this viewpoint the drug abuser and his or her family are caught in a web of relationships that was spun many generations before. The unfortunate patterns are repeated as each new generation depletes the resources of the next. From an intergenerational perspective, the focus is on changing the family relationships. Even when members of previous generations and the extended family are deceased or otherwise unable to participate, their legacies for the person with a drug problem may help unravel the larger pattern of family difficulty.

From an intergenerational family approach Peter's situation is even more complex. Drug abuse in a young adult often serves as a unifying force for the family. In Peter's case, for many years his parents remained together, presenting a strong united front to handle the problem of Peter's drug abuse. At times Peter's addiction was the only thing keeping his parents together. Peter's role had been that of a troublemaker and a seeming failure, but through his failures he made important contributions to the family. He demonstrated loyalty and, paradoxically, cared for his parents by allowing them to work together when his drug abuse caused problems. Now Peter and Janet are beginning to establish the same pattern with their own children.

From an intergenerational perspective, change entails a careful examination of close family relationships. No one is to blame, yet all family members are responsible for improving the situation. In Peter's case he might need to change the relationship with his parents. He might need to find a way to give other than through drug abuse.

What can Peter do to improve his relationship with his father and mother (and vice versa for his parents)? If this improvement in relationships does not happen, then Peter may very well reproduce these same kinds of problems with a spouse, and the problems will continue. Clarifying what family members deserve and owe each other is central to rebalancing intergenerational conflicts that are often at the root of a legacy of substance abuse.

COMMUNITY AND SOCIAL PERSPECTIVE

Finally, if change is thought of in social and community terms, then the community and the society must change in order for the problem of drug abuse to be handled effectively. From this vantage point the larger society is accountable for the drug problem.

One way to bring about change might be for Peter to move to or construct a new community. Peter would be removed from his immediate environment and placed in a *therapeutic community*. Remaining in this new environment usually entails a commitment of two years. The community is oriented toward changing the individual psychologically and is composed of other ex-drug abusers, and counselors, who work daily to confront drug abuse.

We will discuss therapeutic communities more in the chapter on how drug treatment programs work. The point here is that altering the immediate community is one way to bring about change. This approach falls short of actually changing the social environment to which the addicted person will eventually return.

Another way to bring about change from a social and community perspective is to organize politically to change local, state, and national priorities. If Peter's community became organized, with neighbors watching for drug traffic and collaborating with the authorities, then drug abuse would be reduced in that community. It might become more difficult for Peter to get drugs.

Similarly, at a larger level, if society made the elimination of drug abuse its number-one priority, then drug abuse in the form and amount that we see it today would not be possible. Such a change in priorities would require political organization, lobbying, fund raising, and a national network.

LEVELS OF CHANGE INTERACT

These four ways to understand change involve different but complementary points of view: individual, transactional, intergenerational, and community-social. Change may be started from any of these vantage points. It would be a mistake to consider these perspectives in opposition to each other—for example, having to choose between an "individual" and an "intergenerational" approach. One perspective is not better than another. We believe that a family can broaden its scope of vision on the drug problem to expand the range of possible options. In this manner each person can reflect clearly about the problem and develop concrete plans to free themselves from drug abuse. Next, we turn our attention to concepts of the family as a system in more detail.

FAMILY SYSTEMS AND DRUG ABUSE

The notion of the family as a system was actually borrowed from the field of physics. A system may be defined as a set of parts that are connected. The connections between the parts maintain the system as a unit. A key element of systems is a mechanism for feedback. Systems regulate themselves by means of a feedback loop. Individuals, couples, families, communities, and societies all may be described as systems.

A common example of a self-regulatory system is the heating system in a house. As the temperature drops this information is picked up by the thermostat, which triggers a switch connected to the furnace. The furnace is activated, producing more heat, which in turn causes the temperature to rise. As the temperature increases this information is picked up by the thermostat, which deactivates the switch and causes the furnace to shut down. The cycle is repeated again and again as the temperature changes.

We can think of the drug abuser as the family's thermostat for conflict. As the conflict rises the drug abuser precipitates a crisis, generally around drugs, which keeps family members from extreme levels of conflict by making them change focus to the drug abuser's problem. As the drug abuser starts to rehabilitate and do well the family conflict begins to increase again, until the next crisis. All the family members are equally important in the system, and the cycle continues to reproduce itself.

Central to the systemic approach is the idea of nonlinear logic or causality. Linear logic simply means that event A causes B. In our thermostat example, causality is circular (nonlinear). The thermostat (A) causes the switch (B) to turn on the furnace (C) increasing the heat output (D) causing the temperature to rise (E), which causes the thermostat (A) to trip the switch (B) to turn off the furnace (C), and so on. Where we begin and end the sequence of events A, B, C, D, E, A, . . . is arbitrary. Therefore it makes little or no sense to specify which element caused the event. Similarly, in human problems, finding out who is to blame is not the issue. Blaming is linear thinking. The important thing is to recognize the sequence and patterns of action.

MARITAL PATTERNS AND DRUG ABUSE

Family and marital therapists have applied these systems concepts to families with a drug-abusing member. Roy and Myra illustrate a common pattern in a marital system in the following:

Roy: *I've been going out buying drugs with our money. I take money without telling you to go buy it.*

Myra: *You promised you wouldn't smoke coke.*

Roy: *I don't smoke a lot of coke. It's not a problem.*

Myra: *This is just how it was when you were a junkie.*

Roy: *When I used to go get drugs, I didn't come back until I got it. That didn't help our trust thing. That's not happening now.*

Myra: *I never know what's really going on.*

Roy: *You are always saying that, but you hide things from me. You make things seem worse. You exaggerate, thinking I am going to shape up or something. You try to manipulate me—"Do this or else."*

Myra: *I do not.*

Roy: *I know you're afraid that I'll go back to drugs or something, but you've got to be honest with me. You still need to manipulate me in certain ways to get me to do things, and that will not work.*

Myra: *It's not manipulation.*

Roy: *Yes it is.*

Myra: *It's like with the money thing. When I have to sit there and figure out how much money I've earned. How much money you've earned. We are counting our pennies. We are trying to save up. And then you turn around and take money out of my wallet.*

From a systems view, we are not interested in linear causality or with who is right or wrong here. It is more important to examine the pattern of a couple's communication. For example, we might begin the sequence with Roy's statement defending his position of why he took money from Myra. She presses her point by reminding him of his promise. Roy's next statement is to defend himself again. Myra pushes on, almost attacking Roy with the reminder of how he used to be a junkie. Roy denies the accusation, and then Myra's next statement expresses her frustration that she doesn't know anything anymore. At this point Roy turns the table by accusing Myra of manipulating him.

We could start this sequence of events at any point. It would not matter much, because both members of the couple seem stuck on *defending or attacking* each other. Who defends and who attacks could change at any moment.

There are many variations of this type of sequence, which can be seen as "nagger and withdrawer," "pursuer and distancer," "failure and rescuer," or "irresponsible one and caretaker." The individuals in such a couple system are trapped in those roles.

FAMILY OF ORIGIN PATTERNS AND DRUG ABUSE

The defending and attacking roles may be expanded to include three or more people. For example, there is the threesome of persecutor, healer, and victim (or scapegoat). A common pattern is for the father to "persecute" the drug-abusing son, who is often in the role of a "victim." Mother intervenes as a "healer," by both defending and rescuing the son from his father. The pattern often repeats in cycles.

Often these patterns, such as a wife nagging and a husband withdrawing, are connected to unfinished business in the family of origin. Family roles can be passed on from one generation to the next as a means of rebalancing emotional accounts. This hypothetical segment from a marital therapy session with Art and Sally illustrates the intergenerational roots of their marital conflict:

Art: . . . *we are on a tight budget. I knew there should have been some money left. Not a great deal of money, but enough so that I could fill in the gaps* this morning. I knew I would need cigarettes, and there should be money there for it until I could get down to the bank today. And it wasn't there. And I really felt like Sally sits there and she says this and that . . . we discuss things, set a budget, and she goes and takes the money out of my wallet to go out and buy something without telling me. It didn't really matter what she bought. It was just the fact of knowing that there was money there that we needed. Because if I've heard it once, I've heard it twenty times, that things will be different. . . .

Therapist: Let me ask you, do you recognize this as something almost like a pattern with the both of you? That there is the potential for you, Sally, to fail and for you, Art, to rescue her? And for you, Sally, to become more and more seemingly irresponsible?

Sally: There's the potential, but . . .

Therapist: There's the potential in that he becomes the seemingly overly responsible one. . . .

Sally: Yes.

Therapist: And then Art gets to take care of things that you normally should be doing.

Sally: Uh hum.

Therapist: Is this something that has happened to you with other relationships?

Sally: Well . . . in my whole family, my parents to this day don't think I can properly dress myself.

Therapist: You have been the seemingly irresponsible one in your family. Who took care of you then?

Sally: My mother, my father, well, mostly my father. He just takes over everything. Like my husband.

Art: It's now instinctive for me. I'd like to say "OK, fine," and keep my mouth shut. Let her go ahead and do what she is going to do.

Therapist: I am concerned, because I had the idea that you, Sally, have been in a position for a very long time of being seemingly the weak one in your family, the seemingly irresponsible one. And that creates a situation in which someone gets pulled in to take care of you. I think that has been your role for many years. It has been an important role.

The therapist wanted to promote a situation in which Art and Sally could reflect about current behavior patterns in light of their family history. The therapist's interest was in helping the couple identify destructive patterns in their relationship, rather than perpetuating the blaming cycle. Identifying how roles are maintained and transmitted, from the family of origin to the marital situation, is one step toward change. Given that such reflection occurs, the couple may be in a better position to develop a plan of action aimed at changing these patterns and preventing their transmission to future generations.

HOW TO CHANGE FAMILY SYSTEMS

I feel like I am the only one who can help my son stay off drugs, who can help him change. But I feel like I am making things worse.

The old saying "the more things change the more they stay the same" suggests two key elements of change in family systems: (1) stability and persistence; and (2) instability and change. In considering how to change family systems, family therapists often ask themselves what people do to make things stay the same. How has an undesirable situation been maintained unchanged over years? What are the common patterns associated with this problematic situation?

A family member can ask the same question. What does he or she do when there is a crisis around drugs? What do other family members do? Are these actions regular and predictable? Asking these questions can lead to the identification of important family patterns and serve as a useful step toward change.

A second question considered by family therapists concerns what is needed to change things. Related issues involve the risks of change and change in whose interest. Below we discuss guidelines a family member can use to approach the issues of change. First, however, it is important to distinguish two different types of change in family systems.

CHANGE AT DIFFERENT LEVELS

One type of change occurs *inside* the system, leaving the system essentially the same. The other type of change transforms the system itself. For example, consider the transfer of political power in a country where a coup d' état replaces one leader with another, leaving the social system unchanged. This kind of change is "inside" the system. Change transforming the system would be revolutionary in nature—when an altogether different framework of power is created.

At an individual level, think of having a nightmare in which it is impossible to escape from a dangerous situation. Any attempt to change things "inside" the dream—within the framework of the dream—is impossible. Waking up—which involves stepping outside the framework of the dream—would be the second type of change.[2]

Consider this common situation of a family's attempts to change the drug-abusing member. The young woman's drug abuse tends to brings the parents together in joint action to help her. She begins to do better and improve. Then the parents begin to argue, father becomes more distant, and the marriage is threatened. Next the young woman has a relapse, which reinvolves the parents. While the actions of the individuals might change, the basic framework of patterns does not. Here, the more things seem to change the more they remain the same! Changes at the individual level remain changes inside the system. For the problem to be remedied, the framework of family relations must change.

CHANGE IN WHOSE INTEREST?

When we consider change at the level of the family system it is crucial to keep in mind the welfare of all family members. What is in the family's best interest? Who will benefit the most from the desired change? What are the risks of change? By holding onto individual notions of change, a person avoids the complex reality of human conflict, exploitation, and destruction. When we take into account the welfare of more than one person, then we enter another dimension of family relationships.[3] This dimension looks at the balance of fairness in relationships, human rights as well as obligations, entitlements and indebtedness, trust and betrayal.

When we look at two or more sides of a relationship, we can break out of the old one-sided positions and work through conflicting relationships. Considering the welfare of all involved is one important step in bringing about change that is likely to result in building more fairness and trust in family relations. As a general rule, overcoming drug abuse will be in the best interest of the family.

FAMILY AS A RESOURCE

The family is an important resource that is often not fully tapped. A helpful way to approach the issue of change in the family system is, paradoxically, not to try to change the entire family, but instead to change oneself in relationship to the family. Changing the whole family is a complicated project. It requires a more dispassionate perspective than most relatives are used to. As an insider one's vision of how the family system works is limited by the very fact that one is inside the system.

Experience has taught us that if one's goal at the outset is to change one's family or someone else in the family, this will probably fail. People are resistant to efforts to change and may resent the initiator of change, who in turn can get caught in traps. So, what can we do? We can change our own outlook and how *we* behave. The following guidelines for change use the natural resources of the family. They have been derived from research and clinical experience with families in therapy, and we use them in our training program with family members of drug abusers. They are divided into two parts: (1) family patterns and (2) effective communication.

GUIDELINES FOR CHANGE

FAMILY PATTERNS

We get used to relating in particular ways, and often become stuck in them. People assume they know how a person will react to a given situation, because that reaction has happened over and over again. Family members continually try to reach out to each other in ways that do not work. Frustrated, they end up maintaining things as they are.

One way to move toward change in the family is to stand back, identify family patterns, and try to not feed into them. These patterns may be limited to the actions and reactions between two or more people in the family, or they may involve three or more generations. To begin to view the family as an intergenerational system, start by sketching a family tree.

MAKE A FAMILY TREE

Begin by making a family tree or a genealogy of the family (see Chapter 4 for details). We recommend that a family member begin with only the information immediately at hand. Sit down and do as much of the family tree as possible. A study of what is known as well as what is not known is very useful, because the places in which there is little or no information tend to suggest family disconnections or cutoffs. For example, if there is more readily available information about mother's side of the family than about father's side of the family, it is likely that mother's side of the family was more influential.

Once some minimal family information has been recorded, it can be helpful to interview other members about themselves and their history. The information-gathering process itself can help one reconnect to other important family resources. As more information is obtained, the family myths, expectations, disappointments, hardships, and major accomplishments may become clearer. The sum total of these accomplishments and hardships, family debts and merits, constitutes a legacy. Family legacies of loss, emotional deprivation, and indebtedness are often at the root of drug abuse. Clarifying the legacy and learning about one's family history can go a long way toward improving family relationships. To paraphrase Santayana, those who do not understand their family history are likely to repeat it.

EXAMINE FAMILY PATTERNS

Once the tree has been constructed, it can be used to discuss family patterns with others in the family. This will help family members get into a new set of conversations. Identifying recurring patterns through generations can be powerful by itself. People may be living out patterns based on the same recurrent themes that have existed in their family for generations. The following family relationships are typical:

(1) One person shows strength, the other weakness.

Who appears to be in a strong, solid position and who appears to consistently be in a weak position? Contrary to appearances, at times the strong person needs the weak one as much as the weak one needs the strong one. Ironically, the person who appears weak actually holds much strength and power.

(2) One always gives and another always receives.

The drug abuser is in a position of receiving and other family members are in the role of apparently giving. Look for these patterns in other relationships and in other generations. Often one important way to give is to allow others to be constantly giving and taking care of oneself. This is an invisible pattern we have frequently found in families with a serious drug abuse problem.

(3) One is distant, the other pursues.

This pattern is most common in couple relationships. It is as if the couple must maintain a certain "intimate distance" at all times. Thus the more one person pursues, the more the other distances. The more one spouse nags, the more the other withdraws. The more the other withdraws, the more the one nags. The unfortunate pattern keeps repeating itself, although the roles shift at times.

(4) One worries and the other is aloof.

Most families have a "worrier"—the person who always thinks

that "something bad" will happen. Worriers are concerned about important details and things that need to get done. The other side of the coin is the aloof one, who doesn't seem to care or show concern. If the worrier stopped worrying for the family, someone would have to take his or her place. The aloof one might even start to worry.

The drug abuser is often the one to play the aloof role, to be the seemingly irresponsible one. This aloofness begets caretaking and worrying, which is the stance that concerned spouses, parents, and other family members often take in relation to the drug abuser. Ironically, overworrying by family members also begets aloofness and seeming irresponsibility from the drug abuser.

(5) One is the scapegoat, the other is the "knight in shining armor."

The role of scapegoat or the "bad one" may turn into a lifelong mission. Carefully examine family members to discover who seems to be a particularly important failure. Substance abusers are easily identified as scapegoats, bad ones, and often appear side by side with "success" stories or family members who appear to be "knights in shining armor." The brilliance of these success stories is connected to the dishonor of the scapegoat's failures. Each serves to highlight the achievements or failures of the other.

(6) One is the victim, the other a "monster."

Beware of villains and victims. Where there is a "monster" of some kind there is a great potential for improvement and change. In fact, the villains or monsters were often themselves victimized. The "monster" may have perpetrated great injustices, but one way to correct these imbalances is to identify the intergenerational chain of exploitation and begin to work on balancing the debts in people's relations. Victimization and exploitation need to be recognized for what they are, and reparations need to be made. An important focus of work is on preventing further victimization, particularly of the children and future generations.

These patterns can be combined many ways, to include more than two people—even an entire family. These patterns can turn into intergenerational legacies that serve to correct an intergenerational balance of fairness. Seeing how these patterns and missions are played out is important in seeing oneself as part of a larger family story. Based on such information, it may then be possible to develop a plan of action *not* to participate in one's usual role, particularly if what one has been doing seems to be contributing to the problem.

CONNECT WITH UNUSED RESOURCES

As a family member one can call upon relatives one has not spoken with for a long time and ask them for help with the drug problem. Uncles, aunts, grandparents, nieces, nephews, even adult children can be called upon. Families with a drug-abusing member tend to isolate themselves, and it is critical to break through these barriers. A family member does not want anybody else to find out about the problem or may not want to bother people with personal troubles. However, drug abuse is such a common problem that one may find that these family members may have been coping with similar if not the same problems. More often than not, these family members are willing to help, even if this help is only in the form of a sympathetic ear. A family member can call upon a minister or priest, who might be able to provide support, or can make an appointment with a family therapist or other professional oriented toward helping and supporting the family as a whole. Tapping into unused resources gets the family member into an *active* position instead of just reacting to the immediate crisis.

MAKE A TIMELINE OF FAMILY EVENTS

Think about major family events—births, marriages, moves or migrations, divorces, or deaths. Draw a vertical line on a page and list the year for each of these major events. The earliest event in the immediate family might be the date when the parents met. Next list the family members in the family at the time and their ages. Think about the impact the event had on each family member. How did they respond to the event?

In reviewing the family chronology, think about the wider social and community context. For example, during the 1960s and 1970s young men and women freely experimented with all sorts of drugs. It is important to make a note of social developments of this type. Perhaps the family moved to another part of the nation or the family migrated to another country. Migrations of any kind tend to be rather disruptive for families. Other events of family significance might include war, unemployment, economic recession or depression, a natural disaster, or a serious illness.

To understand the impact of an event on a family member, ask not only about the event but also about how people were affected by it. Making a family chronology helps to put the family in context and serves as a means to appreciate the family as a system. Often ideas, images, and emotions developed when we were children continue to dominate our lives. A chronology of events might help us to view these same images from the perspective of an adult. It may be helpful to think about how different people responded to the events given their ages, their development, and social limitations.

WORK ON FAMILY LOSSES

Families with drug abuse problems also tend to have had major issues of loss, as explained in Chapter 4. Talk about the loss together with the family. This might help with mourning. By accepting and facing the loss, ghosts may be laid to rest and the family members released to live richer lives.

EFFECTIVE COMMUNICATION

One way to initiate change in relationships is to change one's habits of talking or communicating.[5] In family relations we often find ourselves talking and relating in the same old ways, assuming others will also respond predictably. This discussion goes nowhere. Below we outline several ways to approach change in how people communicate and relate to each other.

USE "I" STATEMENTS

We often blame the other in conversation—"You make me feel so bad! How can you hurt me like this?" But this accusatory stance only serves to make the other person defensive. Use of "I" statements can change this pattern by freeing the other of blame. For example, the conversation above could be restated: "I really feel bad when we argue like this. I'm hurt when you come home so late." Try not to talk about someone else, but just about oneself. Thus one can clarify one's own needs, wishes, and limits without making accusations. The use of "I" statements can help sort out what one deserves and is entitled to in a relationship.

RECOGNIZE BLAMING AND DON'T PARTICIPATE

The process of blaming and counterblaming is one of the most destructive aspects of communication.[4] A family member who is involved in a blaming cycle must first try to recognized it for what it is. Generally, these are attacks and counterattacks that are repetitive and have no tangible outcome except the emotional depletion of both the family member and the person with the drug problem. For example, Mary: "You spent all my money again!" Dan: "You never give me enough!" Mary: "Well if you worked, maybe we'd have more!" And so on.

Second, try to get out of the cycle either by talking about how both family members got into blaming each other again or by talking about oneself. Here is where a person can use "I statements." Talk about personal disappointments, perhaps, but state them as one's own with no blame attached. Doing this halts the blaming cycle.

CREATE ADULT RELATIONSHIPS WITH FAMILY MEMBERS

This is difficult, but one way to move toward more adult relationships with family members is to develop one-to-one (dyadic) relationships. Within families we often develop a pattern of relating by talking about a third person ("John's stoned again.") It is natural to engage in family gossip; but think what the relationship would be like if "John" was not there to say bad things about? One way to get into one-to-one relationships is to write letters or set up activities that exclude a third person. For example, one of the authors started calling his father at work so that he could have a conversation without his mother at the other end of the line. If one involves other family members in the search for family genealogy, this might also help to avoid the usual topics of conversation.

One can look at spouse, parents, siblings, and grown children as mature adults with whom one can be a responsible, caring adult. In this process family members discover what is owed to them in the family and what can be given now.

DON'T ATTACK, DEFEND, OR WITHDRAW

These are key behaviors to avoid. An attack invites defense and argument. Defending one's viewpoint invites attack. Withdrawal from the relationship is a punishment of oneself as well as one's loved one. By avoiding these three don'ts, relationships will be more creative.

DON'T TOLERATE EMOTIONAL BLACKMAIL

If family members accept such threats as, "If you don't do this for me, I'll kill myself" or "I'll go get high" or "I'll withdraw my love," they will be trapped in a reactive position. In these situations it is most important to make oneself available to the person in need by clearly defining limits. Of course, life-threatening situations must be taken seriously. Calling for professional advice or the authorities may be necessary if someone's life is actually at risk. Nevertheless, emotional blackmail cannot be tolerated if one's goal is to improve the relationship. A relationship based on emotional blackmail is exploitative and doomed to failure.

That "no man is an island" is a truism known to most of us. Yet we live in a society where the individual is glorified and, perhaps, overemphasized. When problems arise, we tend to blame the individual. Individually conceived solutions often fail because we are *not* islands distant and insulated from each other. Rather, we are part of a complex social context, highly dependent on each other. Our actions and reactions form patterns in a web of family and social relations which are part of a greater whole. Often a different way of understanding drug problems and generating solutions can go a long way in resolving problems, producing change, and improving family relations.

Adopting a family perspective can serve as an important resource to understand and overcome drug abuse. Through the family prism the meaning of change can be understood from different vantage points. In this chapter we examined individual, transactional, intergenerational, and community perspectives to understand and combat drug abuse. All of these approaches and interventions may be necessary to cope effectively with drug addiction.

Change begins at home, and with oneself. Family members who are willing to look at family processes and patterns will be in a better position to prevent drug abuse. Change, as we have learned, involves reflection linked to action. Taking preventive and corrective action in one's own family will strengthen the family position and increase its effectiveness in working toward mobilizing resources and producing change at the social and community level.

6. Saying "No" to Drugs and Building Motivation

SAYING "NO" TO DRUG ABUSE

The trouble is, I can't say "no." One time I even went with him to buy drugs. So there I am down in the middle of the drug-selling district, asking myself, "What am I doing here?"

The person who is close to a family member with a drug problem often must decide to say "yes" or "no" to requests. Everyone gets put in these situations once in a while, but the dramatic nature of the drug abuser's problems makes the situations more intense. The family member feels pulled between saying "yes" and saying "no." Drug abusers may have many reasons why they need a person to say "yes," and the family member knows he or she will feel badly about denying them what they want; however, there is still an uneasy feeling about it. Is it best to say "yes"? The family member worries about other consequences. For example, by lending the drug abuser money is the family member encouraging him or her to borrow from others regularly rather than learning to live within a budget? This section of the chapter deals with being able to say "no" when one feels pressure to say "yes."

NOT SAYING "NO" CAN BE A PROBLEM

I was pretty sure my friend was using drugs again. She asked me to come to a party where I thought there would be drugs. She asked me to drive, and it was far away. I didn't want to, but . . .

For a person who cannot say "no," life is filled with frustration. This is true for drug abusers and for family members alike. *Not* saying "no" can distract us from what we really want to do. As one woman said to us: "I'm soft-hearted, I guess . . . I can never say "no." Even my best girlfriend says, 'You should live your own life.' "

When we can't say "no," resentment builds. We feel like we are being used. Friends want us for our car, others want us for our paycheck—that is not a good way to build relationships. Eventually, a person who can't say "no" gets upset about the situation:

My cousin is a heroin addict. He stayed at my apartment for three weeks when I was on vacation. He used my place as a shooting gallery—all his junkie friends were doing drugs there. I returned to find blood droplets on the bathroom floor, cotton wads in the wastebaskets, and my cousin saying, "I'm clean." When I went to pay my bills for the month, many of my checks were missing. Later all of my checks bounced because some had been forged. Finally I cut off ties with my cousin. I decided I would no longer be manipulated and used, lied to, cheated, and robbed.

By not saying no a person can get led into doing things that produce guilty feelings. This frequently happens with the person who is trying to recover from drug problems. The individual does not want to get involved with drugs again, but it is very hard to say no when drugs have been a major part of friendships and social life. A friend may ask the recovering drug abuser over for the afternoon to listen to music, but as the day goes on the person finds himself or herself being led into old habits that are later regretted.

Finally, one of the biggest problems with not knowing how to say "no" is that other people do not understand what an individual really wants. They think that the person likes being "easy," that the person likes pleasing them rather than pleasing himself or herself. They have no idea what it is that the person really wants.

REASONS ARE NOT ALWAYS OBVIOUS

My son and daughter-in-law asked me to babysit for them so that they could go out. I knew that they would be with old friends who are involved with drugs. I love the kids, and I love the grandkids. I don't want to help set them up to get in trouble, but . . .

Why would the grandmother in this example have a difficult time saying no? Sometimes it is a desire to avoid confrontation, not being liked, or losing someone. In this way it can be easier to say no to people at work, where there are lines separating one's personal life from the lives of the people one works with. Losing a family member, however, can have drastic consequences, so it is harder to say "no."

Other times it is a matter of not wanting someone to get the wrong idea. A mother does not want her children to think she is a poor parent, or impolite, or she does not want to look stupid or selfish in their eyes. Sometimes she may feel she is not entitled to say "no." "Who am I to say no? After all, they asked me to babysit; they have a right to my services. Besides, I want to help my children." Sometimes people mistake saying yes with being helpful and think if they say no they must be hurting someone. In our experience, people with drug problems often hope that a family member will set limits for them. They want someone to say no, or they want someone to say, "That's a stupid thing for you to do, and I won't help you with it."

WAYS TO SAY "NO" EFFECTIVELY

Elaine: *It's very difficult, when I always give in at the end. By the twentieth time I'm in trouble.*

Carol: *Once you stand your ground a couple of times it can be easier. It helps if you have support too. After some time they'll get the message. Hang in there. I've done it, but it's hard.*

The final reason for not saying "no" is the most frequent one —a person just does not know how. The first rule in learning how to say "no" is to be persistent: Say what is wanted over and over and over again, without getting angry or irritated or loud. Be firm and brief. There is no need to state a reason or an excuse.

BROKEN RECORD TECHNIQUE

Bob and Jack want to borrow my car to go out next Saturday night. I don't really feel like lending my car to them, but they're my good friends . . .

The technique of being persistent is sometimes called the "broken record" technique, meaning that an individual says "no" over and over and over again, as if the needle of a personal record player was stuck. For example, with the close friends who want to borrow the car:

No, you can't borrow my car. I know you'll take good care of it, but no, you can't borrow my car. Why? Why doesn't matter: No, you can't borrow my car. I know you have a date, but no, you can't borrow my car.

Eventually, they will get the idea that no, they cannot borrow the car on Saturday night. This technique is useful when a person is being asked to say "yes" about something that is under personal control, for example, personal loans of money or possessions.

MAKE IT CLEAR THAT IT'S THEIR PROBLEM

Anyone can avoid inheriting the world's problems, simply by not accepting them. For example, not agreeing to take on others' problems might work well for the grandmother whose son and daughter-in-law asked her to babysit so that they could go out with friends who are using drugs. One way to respond to that request is to make it clear that the problem belongs not to the grandmother, but to the parents:

You have a problem. You need a babysitter for Saturday night, but it's not going to be me. I know that those are lovely children, and they would be easy for me to take care of. But you have the problem. The children are your responsibility, not mine. Whether or not I have anything planned for Saturday night is not the issue. The issue is that they are your children, and I'm not going to babysit them Saturday night. I know that you think you are very strong and think you will not get involved with drugs at the party. But I am not so sure of that, and I know that I'm not going to babysit for you. The problem is yours—you need the babysitter, not me.

THE FOGGING TECHNIQUE

My parents have been calling me every day this week. They're being real nags. They keep asking, "When did you say you were coming over this weekend? You don't spend enough time with the family."

One can agree with the problem without having to give in to something that is undesirable. For example, in coping with the parents who have been calling every day this week, even when their son had not agreed to come over at all this weekend:

I agree, folks. I don't spend enough time with the family. But, I'm not coming over this weekend. Maybe that is a really insensitive thing for me to do, but I'm not coming over. I know you'll be really lonely and don't know what you'll do with yourselves, but I'm not coming over.

This technique is called "fogging." In San Francisco, where the authors reside, on some nights fog is everywhere. We can take our umbrellas and push at it, spear it, or run through it, but we cannot get rid of the fog. It surrounds us. That is the technique used in fogging. A person agrees with the problem but does *not* agree to be the solution to it. Fogging is a good technique to use when people nag, because when people nag they are expecting resistance. *Agreeing with the problem disarms them.* It is also frequently used by an employee with the boss, because it provides a way for the worker to hold ground while not challenging the authority of the boss.

I NEED TO SAY "NO"

Sometimes a family member can simply take personal responsibility for the decision: "I'm not going to lend you my car because I don't want to worry about the two of you getting into trouble. I don't want to risk feeling bad. If you did get into trouble, no matter what the circumstances, I would feel responsible." The family member acknowledges the other's point of view, but clearly takes a personal stand. In short, the family member decides on his or her personal limits, and takes responsibility for them.

WHEN TO COMPROMISE

One disadvantage of these techniques is that they can build up walls between people. Using a technique sets up a psychological barrier, because one is putting some distance between oneself and others.

Why should a family member use one of these techniques to say "no?" Because one's self-respect is at stake. If disagreement can be settled on the merits of the case rather than on the basis of who has the stronger personality, then it is possible to reach a workable compromise.

Compromise can give people what they need while protecting the family member's interests. Both sides feel good about the process, because they are working together rather than against each other. For example, consider the person who was asked to attend a party where there would be drugs and was asked to drive. A workable compromise would be to explain one's concern about falling back into drug use again, and instead to invite the other person over for the evening. For the grandmother whose son and daughter-in-law asked her to babysit, a workable compromise might be for the grandmother to say no to this, but also say that she knows they need some time alone and some recreation, so she would be happy to take the kids to the zoo the next day.

A compromise will not work if the other side will not be reasonable. If they are trying to overwhelm the family member with their needs or are so desperate that they do not care about the feelings of others, then a family member can consider using one of the techniques above to simply say "no."

WHY SAY "NO"?

Saying "no" is particularly important in a family where there is a drug problem. It is a way to take care of drug abusers by setting limits. In addition, it can free a family member to be an individual and not the person of someone else's dreams. Saying "no" can allow a person to communicate with others in an open, direct, and honest way. Saying "no" can serve to satisfy the family member's needs and respect the family member's point of view.[1]

When drug abuse is involved, saying "no" is especially difficult. The very lives of drug-abusing family members may be precariously hanging between a drug habit, dangerous friends, and countless scrapes with the authorities. The family member feels pulled to ease the pressure on the drug user by saying "yes." A mother of a drug abuser says, "I'm afraid that he'll end up like those people I see down on skid row if I don't help." A wife says, "I've threatened to leave him, but he says he will kill himself." The point in the first part of this chapter is that a family member can decide whether or not to say "yes." The family member can examine the consequences, and decide whether or not the family is willing to pay the price of saying "yes." When in doubt, the family member can keep in mind that nice people *can* say "no."

A family member can say "no" by being direct and being persistent (the "broken record" technique). Another technique is to clarify responsibilities ("It's your problem, not mine"). A family member can say "no" by understanding the others' point of view without giving in (the "fogging" technique), or by stating one's personal need to do so. Finally, a family member can say "no" by working out a compromise if the disagreement can be setteled on the basis of the merits of the case rather than on the basis of who is better at arguing. In other words it can be useful to compromise, but every family member has the right to say "no."

BUILDING MOTIVATION

Building motivation is in many ways the opposite of saying "no." A family member can stop a negatively motivated person by saying "no." But another aspect is just as important: helping drug abusers to say "yes" to help and possibilities.

He has talents, but how can I motivate him to develop them? . . . She never takes responsibility and therefore is going nowhere. . . . He seems motivated to fail. . . . She does not know what she wants in life. . . . He seems unreliable and does not follow through responsibly.

How can a family member help the drug abuser build a true motivation to succeed? New parents learn early that they cannot simply take a rattle away from their baby; instead they must replace the rattle in the baby's hand with something else. This is one of the universal principles: *Nature abhors a vacuum.* It also applies to drug abuse: Drug abusers must say "no" to drugs, but they must also replace the drugs with something else. Giving up drugs involves (1) giving up a substance that makes them feel good (which must be replaced by something that makes them feel good about themselves); (2) saying "no" to drug dealing or criminality (which must be replaced by an honest way of making a living); and (3) cutting ties with drug-involved friends (and finding new friends who are not connected to the drug world). It is important for the drug user to find other ways to feel good, to seek job opportunities, and to find a new set of friends. In short, to begin living a normal life. Saying "no" is only half the fight.

It is crucial for the drug abusers to replace motivation for drug use with a motivation for recovery. If they do not they will fail, even though they may make other apparent progress.

COMMON PROBLEMS

Holding Up One's End of the Partnership

At the store I acted like nothing was going on. I mean I tried to maintain a normal life and then go home and deal with someone who is a drug addict and who would constantly say, "Well, I'm going to change."

I really was there as support, and I think I'm a strong person. I got to the point where I said, "Hell, do I have to be this strong? I mean, why do I have to be the caretaker? I'd just as soon have somebody take care of me."

It is common in marital relationships for the spouse to feel that the drug abuser is not holding up his or her end of the marital partnership. When one person is weak, the other acts as the strong one. These roles can be difficult to give up. As the weak one becomes stronger, the strong one becomes weaker. Sometimes people even reverse roles.

One former drug abuser explained it this way. While he was "using," his wife did it all—took care of food, laundry, paying bills, social life. When he stopped using drugs he tried to take responsibility for more tasks around the house. As he did this she became unable to take care of things that she *had* been doing. "All of a sudden she wanted me to take care of *her,"* he said, "and I couldn't do that." He began to use drugs again.

This kind of marital imbalance takes place not just with partners in "strong-weak" relationships, but with those in "pursuer-distancer" roles and "monster-victim" roles also. Change is frightening. It seems safer to stay locked in unhappy roles that are at least familiar to both parties. The problem, then, is how to change roles in a way that helps the drug abuser to live "clean" without destroying the marital relationship.

MOTIVATED TO FAIL

My sister was doing so well this time. She came to live with me, and we got her into treatment. She was even going to get her children back to live with her in her own apartment. Then that man came, the man who got her started in it all, and she just blew it. She was gone, back using drugs again.

Frequently people with drug problems will seem to be making progress, and then they will relapse for no apparent reason. They throw away months or even years of painfully won gains. They are so adept at messing up that they are known for being experts at failure.

The family member is in a peculiar position. By rescuing drug abusers family members reward them for failure. For example, a father who pays for his daughter's bad checks is protecting the daughter; but by not allowing the daughter to suffer the consequences of her misbehavior he is also rewarding her for acting irresponsibly. The same process occurs in other situations, where the drug abuser fails to pay the rent and is in danger of eviction, gets fired from a job and asks for support, or is about to be expelled from school. There is a narrow path between offering support to people in need (which is, of course, a loving thing to do) and helping them to stay involved with drugs by giving rewards for drug-involved failure. For this reason the family member is often uncertain about how to prevent drug abusers from being motivated to fail.

CONFUSED ABOUT DIRECTIONS

As part of the recovery process, drug abusers enter a new world. If they are teens they may not know the kind of life they want to live or the kind of jobs they can hold. If they are more experienced, they have been living in a drug-using world foreign to the family. A family member who wants to help them get used to living comfortably in the non-drug world may not know how. A wife, for example, may worry that her husband's friends are influencing him to continue a directionless life of substance abuse, but she does not know how to turn him away from these negative influences.

A parent is naturally more concerned about direction than other family members. For example, a father holds a long-term concern about his daughter's welfare. He sees that his daughter is associating with the wrong crowd, leading to confusion about her identity. The father may find it difficult to let go because of a fear that his daughter, left on her own, will continue a pattern of failure and drug abuse. As a parent he feels that he can help his daughter, but is frustrated because he knows that the motivation needs to come from her.

LACK OF TRUST

Trust is a crucial issue for a family member, whether parent, spouse, sibling, or child of drug abusers. When drug abusing family members are "using," they might not be trusted even with simple tasks. When she goes to the grocery store she might not bring back any change, or she might not come back for a long, long time. The parent has questions about the amount of support or supervision needed. The spouse needs to know whether or not the partnership can ever be as it was (at least in expectations) at the beginning of their relationship. For the child of a drug abuser, trust is a vital issue in identity formation. Once former drug abusers are recovering, the issue becomes how to rebuild trust with the family. One woman whose fiancé had been a heroin addict said: "Can I ever trust him again, given the number of times he has let me down?"

A PROBLEM-SOLVING MODEL

Motivation problems are complicated and cannot be solved overnight. Nevertheless, a general model for problem-solving can be useful in a variety of situations. This model has been used for years by counselors and psychologists for treating other difficulties, and it applies especially well to the family member coping with drug abusers' motivation.[2] The model that the authors use involves taking six steps: (1) identifying the problem, (2) generating alternative solutions, (3) selecting one solution to try, (4) rehearsing, (5) trying it, and (6) evaluating.

1. IDENTIFY THE PROBLEM

The key concept in changing motivation is understanding that an individual cannot change others but can only change his or her personal relationship with them. A person can say "no," but cannot *make others* say yes. Consequently, it is crucial to redefine each motivational issue in terms of a family member's relationship to a person with drug problems. It is not that the drug user is irresponsible; instead, the problem is that he or she is not holding up his or her end of the relationship. The problem is not that they are untrustworthy; instead, the problem is that the family member cannot trust them with things that everyone cares about. The family member cannot change them, but can affect the personal *relationship* directly.

In one of our sponsor training sessions the sponsors included a client's brother, another client's close friend, and a fiance who lived with a client. When we asked about problems related to the drug user's motivation, or lack of it, several examples emerged. The brother complained that the client blamed everything on him.

The close friend complained that the client always had great plans, but he never seemed to follow through on them, even though he wanted people to take him seriously. The fiancé, Kyle, complained that his woman somehow always made things *his* problem. This last issue touched the rest of the group, and we identified a problem in the relationship—Kyle felt like he was being responsible, but the drug abuser was not. All wished that she would be more responsible. Whether or not the drug abuser was irresponsible in other parts of her life, the key was that she was not responsible in her relationship with Kyle. Thus the problem was identified as something between two people, and hence something that Kyle could affect directly. He could stop taking responsibility for his fiancée's mistakes.

2. GENERATE ALTERNATIVE SOLUTIONS

Once the motivational issue has been identified in terms of an interpersonal relationship, the key is for the family member to think of as many ways as possible to change the relationship with drug abusers in the family. A person can get help in this by working in a group, getting the assistance of a friend, or holding a family meeting to discuss how the problem might be addressed. It is wise to list all the alternatives suggested, even if they seem to be poor ideas at the time. Then the family member can go back to them later if the best-sounding ideas do not seem to be working.

In Kyle's case, the problem was that the drug abuser was not being responsible in her relationship with Kyle, her lover. The group generated a number of alternatives that Kyle could try with her:

1. *Give her tasks to do,* like going to the grocery store for milk or doing things around the house that you normally would do for her.
2. *Ask her to do things.* Don't just let her irresponsibility slide.
3. *Confront her* with the issue directly.
4. *Discuss it* with her.
5. *Test her* by giving little tasks that, if handled well, can lead

to more responsibility. As one sponsor said, "It's not that the little things are important, but when the little things are being taken care of, you figure that the big things are OK too."

6. *Lower your sights.* Expect that this is the kind of relationship that you will have, and live with it.

7. *Let her lead.* Let her see that things won't be taken care of unless she is more responsible.

8. *Shame her.* For example, "I am losing respect for you."

9. Try *"bank shots".* This means talking to the client about someone else who has a problem similar to that of the client.

10. *Set an example* for her, but don't harp on it.

11. *Yell* when you are frustrated with her.

12. *Threaten.* For example, threaten to leave her.

13. *Dump her.* Stop trying to make a bad situation workable.

The solutions were not all compatible, but Kyle appreciated the efforts of the group to help. He had tried several of the ideas. Some of the suggestions, however, were ones he had never considered even though they fit well with his way of interacting with the drug abuser.

3. SELECT ONE SOLUTION TO TRY

How does a family member decide which solution to attempt? A first step is to ask which solutions bear directly on the problem. For example, in the list above solution 10—set an example—does not get directly at the problem of the drug abuser's irresponsibility in the relationship, and so it is not optimal. The same is true of trying "bank shots" (solution 9).

A second question to ask is which solutions are most feasible. That is, which can be tried within a relatively short time? The family member is changing not just the drug abuser, but him or herself too. Whatever is tried needs to be something that can be done comfortably. To have a chance at being successful, a family member will need to at least try the solution to see if it will have an effect. One can start with a simple, small action that will give confidence to try more dramatic solutions if they are needed. In the list above, for example, it may not be feasible for Kyle to threaten to leave his fiancée (solution 13) if Kyle has hopes for their future.

Kyle selected "bank shots" (solution 9) because that seemed to be the most creative solution that was relatively easy and non-threatening for him to try. He felt that some of the others would require him to act like the drug abuser's parent (solutions like giving her tasks [1] or testing her [5]) or to raise the issue more bluntly (solutions that involved talking with her [4], confrontation [3] or threats [12]), which was not his way of doing things.

From the viewpoint of an outsider this may not seem to be the best solution—it does not directly affect the responsibility issue. Nevertheless, it is good to keep in mind that you have a number of options, and if one does not work you can try another. It is most important to know that you are doing *something* about the problem, rather than letting the motivational issue fester. In this case "bank shots" was a technique that Kyle had not heard of before, and the person suggesting it was an ex-addict who demonstrated it vividly for the group. Kyle thought that, if he could use it, the technique would be really useful.

4. REHEARSE

It may be helpful to talk through the planned discussion, preferably with another person. If no one else is available, a person can still rehearse the situation by talking in front of a mirror or just by thinking all the way through the scene. Having someone to talk with can take away the tenderness of the issue for a family member. The two people can act out the situation to explore different ways to introduce the issue. Often this role playing will be harder than the real thing, but done in a safer setting that prepares the family member for the actual situation. The two can rehearse what the family member will say, with the other person playing the role of the drug abusing family member. Then they can reverse roles, so that the family member can understand how the drug abuser is likely to view the situation. Rehearsal can help one gain a new perspective on the situation, and it will ease the family member into actually trying the solution that has been selected.

Kyle was hesitant about rehearsing the delivery of "bank shots." Sylvie volunteered to demonstrate how she used the technique with her son, who had a problem with alcohol. Sylvie asked Kyle to play the drug abuser, who is in the same room while his mother is talking with someone.

Sylvie then commented to her friend:

Oh, your daughter has a problem with alcohol. That's too bad. I can imagine what it is like, when you, her mother, are up late at night. You are worried about what's happening to your daughter, so you wish she would get home. But at the same time you dread what will happen when she does get home and might be intoxicated or high. That's hard on a mother when her child has a problem with alcohol or drugs.

Kyle listened to Sylvie deliver the bank shots and liked the technique.

5. TRY THE SOLUTION

The family member can choose a time and situation to act, and change the relationship in the way planned. Timing can be important—one does not want to let an opportunity slide past, nor to "ambush" drug-abusing family members with material that they will not be able to absorb or that will lead to their rejecting both the solution and the family member. It is wise to plan the length of time to try the solution, using it in a trial period to see how well the action is working. If the family member views the solution as temporary it will be easier to try. The family member can always return to the old way of doing things.

If the goal is to help the drug abuser understand more about the relationship, then the family member should choose a quiet setting. In a place where each person has an opportunity to express feelings about their relationship, the family member can bring up the issue then give the drug abuser time to hear what has been said. Then solutions are suggested. However, if the goal is to change the drug abuser's *behavior,* as opposed to understanding, then it may be wisest for the family member to simply implement the change rather than talk about it.

Kyle attempted a "bank shot" as a way to change his fiancée's irresponsibility, but he was unhappy in the role. He told her one of the stories he had heard in sponsor training, about how a husband had been embarrassed to learn from the landlord that they owed a month's rent, even though the husband had given the rent money to his wife to be paid. Kyle related,

It went right over her head, and she didn't let me finish the story. I felt really uncomfortable trying to lead her to insight. The whole thing felt artificial.

6. EVALUATE

This is a key step in the problem-solving model. Is the solution working? Is the relationship with the drug abusers changing in the way planned? If so, then the family member can extend the length of the trial period, or the number of situations in which the solution is tried. If altering the solution seems futile, the family member can go back to the original list of possible solutions and select another to rehearse.

Kyle didn't know why, but his "bank shots" solution had flopped completely. The group helped him analyze why the solution had not been successful. It seemed to most that "bank shots" were difficult to use with his woman, and a better solution would need to be simpler and more direct. Kyle decided to abandon "bank shots" for now.

Kyle selected a new approach, giving his fiancée a task that he would normally do for them. Kyle decided to ask his fiancée to go do the shopping, and with another group member he rehearsed a way to ask her to go. He would tell his fiancée that he felt overloaded and simply couldn't do so many things for them. He wanted her to help out by going to the supermarket and buying their food for the week. He would give a list and money enough to cover the purchases.

7. PROBLEMS WITH PROBLEM SOLVING

Frequently, trying a solution will have unintended effects, and the family member will need to decide whether or not to change the approach. One father of a drug abuser in our sponsor training program for example, tried a solution one week and came back feeling confused. The problem was unclear communication between him and his daughter, and the solution he chose was to point out the pattern. He rehearsed it in the group and chose a time and situation to bring it up. When he tried it with his daughter, however, he got more than he bargained for. His daughter *did* change the problem behavior, but their conversation became emotional, building to her saying: "You don't know me, Dad. You think you do, but I'm not the person you think I am. You really don't know me at all." He felt uncomfortable, not knowing whether or not to wade deeper into these waters. This was a part of their relationship that he had not been prepared to discuss.

Should a family member attempt more than one solution at a time? It depends on the problem and the person's experience with problem solving. In attempting to change motivation, usually the situation is not desperate, and if the problem-solving approach is new, a family member is probably best advised to take things a step at a time. However, if the situation is life threatening or the relationship with the drug abuser is deteriorating rapidly, the family member may want to implement several solutions at once. In Kyle's situation, for example, he could confront his fiancée on several levels, threatening to cut off their relationship if she did not improve, giving her tasks to do, shaming her, and responding openly with his frustration each time she acted irresponsibly. The combination of these approaches would certainly get his fiancée's attention and is likely to have an impact, but it is much more work for both of them and could endanger other parts of their relationship.

Kyle tried the "give her tasks" solution with some success. His fiancée did the grocery shopping but could not find two items, and with some items she came back with the wrong size. She improved in later trips, and he was relieved to have her help in this area of their life.

Unfortunately, her drug abuse worsened later, and she became even more irresponsible. Sometimes she was not around when it was time to go shopping, on another occasion she "lost" the grocery money. Kyle escalated his efforts—confronting her about not following through. In the end he broke off their engagement and left her when her irresponsibility became intolerable.

Reflecting on the efforts at motivating his fiancée Kyle felt grateful for the support of the group and the problem-solving model.

They gave me something to hang on to when I felt like she was making me crazy. It felt like either she was way off or I was . . . and when that happened I'd go back to evaluating and rehearsing and trying again in a different way. I kept wishing that she would change, but I was working at it harder than she was. Finally we were both so unhappy that I just couldn't live with it anymore.

The most important part in motivating others is keeping one's own spirits up—motivating the motivator. There are no easy solutions in changing other people's motivations. In changing one's relationship to them a family member is changing him or herself as well.

Every family member of a drug abuser has a secret hope that one day the problem will simply go away. Like fog lifting off a landscape the problem will dissipate, and the person will be cured. That is not the way things work with drug problems. People give up drugs because they change their situation, or they see that continuing their drug use will deprive them of other things (or people) more important to them, or because they get motivated to do other things. The family can help in that process, but it is hard work that is likely to require repetition many times. Drug abusers are not likely to thank the family member for these efforts (although their changed motivation is likely to be reward enough). It is important to get some support *for the family member,* which can come from other family members or from some of the professionals and self-help groups for families that are explained later in this book. Change is difficult, and a family member will be better off with a group that supports these efforts.

Kyle's experience provides a realistic example of making an effort to motivate a drug abuser. By defining her irresponsibility in terms of their relationship, Kyle could attack the problem without attacking his fiancée's character. His first efforts at "bank shots" did not succeed, but by evaluating and refining his techniques he produced some change. When her irresponsibility worsened later, he escalated his efforts appropriately. Although we can debate whether or not he should have cut off the relationship when he did, Kyle took that action with the understanding that the problem was his as well as hers. (There is an excellent book entitled *Quitting: Knowing When to Leave,* which provides sage guidance for people who are unsure whether or not to continue a relationship.[3]) In Kyle's case he could not change her motivation to a level acceptable to him, but he could change his relationship to the drug abuser.

THE FAMILY'S RESPONSIBILITY

If one changes the way one relates to drug abusers in the family, life can be less trying, and the drug problem will be more likely to be defeated. Learning to say "no" is part of that change. Not every family member has the problem of being too "easy," but many family members do. The drug abuser quickly gravitates to the "easy" person. Such people can benefit from learning when and how to be tougher.

Another part of the change is helping the drug abusing family members to be motivated—to take advantage of opportunities in the "clean" world. This chapter focused on how to analyze the problem in terms of a family member's relationship to drug abusers, so that the family can work on problems directly. Success is not certain, but by using this model the person will know what he or she is trying to do, and how well the goals are being accomplished. Change is always difficult, but by continuing to make efforts the family member can influence the likelihood of recovery. A family member's relationship to drug abusers is something the family *can* change, and that relationship can influence the likelihood that drug abusing family members will recover. However, although a family member can help to provide opportunities for recovery, ultimately drug abusing family members are responsible for their own lives.

III. RESOURCES FOR THE FAMILY

7. Recognizing the Signs of Drug Abuse

Therapist: *If he was using drugs would you know it at the time?*

Dawn: *No, I was pretty dumb about that . . . but I didn't know as much about it as I do now.*

How can one know when drug use is getting out of hand? A family member is in an excellent position to detect emerging drug problems, because the family is both physically and emotionally close to the user and can tell when his or her behavior is changing. To detect problems, however, the family member needs to be aware of the signs of drug abuse.

First, the reader must understand that there is a fine line between "using" and "abusing" a drug. An emotionally involved family member may not find it easy to tell the difference between use and abuse. Second, a family member can recognize the signs. A family member can learn to detect when a person is "loaded," in withdrawal, or troubled by substance abuse. Third, once one is confident about recognizing the signs and telling the difference between drug use and abuse, family members and friends of the family can be quite helpful in resolving the problems.

DIAGNOSING THE PROBLEM

THE DIFFERENCES BETWEEN DRUG USE AND ABUSE

Unfortunately, the line between drug use and abuse is usually not clear. For example, the continuum of alcohol use in Figure 6 illustrates the complex patterns associated with alcohol usage. A moderate social drinker is not much different from a heavy social drinker, and that person is not much different from a careless drinker. The line in the middle of the page, dividing "social" from

Figure 6

The Problem Drinking Continuum

DEATH FROM ALCOHOLISM

DRINKING BEHAVIOR: Patterns of Use and Abuse

⇦	SOCIAL ⇨		Heavy ⇨
Light	Moderate		

Drinks less than once per month

1–3 drinks per occasion

Intoxicated several times in life

Drinks 1–4 times per month

1–3 drinks per occasion

"High" several times per year

Drunk 1–4 times in life

Drinks 1–7 times per week

1–6 drinks per occasion

"High" weekly

Drunk once per month

NO DRINKING

CARELESS ⇨

When you drink, you
DRINK TOO MUCH

Minor Problems

Family—quarrels, arguments
Job—occasional missed work
Money—insurance rates, fines
Law—one arrest
Sex—impaired performance
Hang-overs that interfere with activities
Embarrassment about things done while drinking

PROBLEM AREA ⇨

PROBLEM ⇨

Inability to consistently predict amount, frequency, duration, and/or the effect of drinking.

Addiction
    Changes in tolerance
    Withdrawal effects
    Morning drinks, the "eye-opener"
    Shakes, neglect of food
Sneaking drinks, lies, excuses
Frequent blackouts
Benders or binges
Severe health problems—hospitalization

More severe problems:

Several arrests—legal problems
Family complains about drinking
Separation, divorce
Missed work or lost jobs
Belligerence, arguments, fights, injury
Money problems, unpaid bills
Impotence, frigidity
Health problems

Drinking alone or at inappropriate time

BLACKOUTS

Increase in tolerance

Relief drinking—to relax, calm down, sleep, nerves

ALCOHOLIC ⇨

NO PROBLEMS RELATED TO DRINKING

YOU DO NOT HAVE TO BE AN "ALCOHOLIC"
TO HAVE A DRINKING PROBLEM

REVERSIBLE PHYSIOLOGICAL DAMAGE—LIVER, STOMACH, PANCREAS, SKIN, HEART

IRREVERSIBLE PHYSIOLOGICAL DAMAGE
LIVER, BRAIN, STOMACH, PANCREAS, HEART

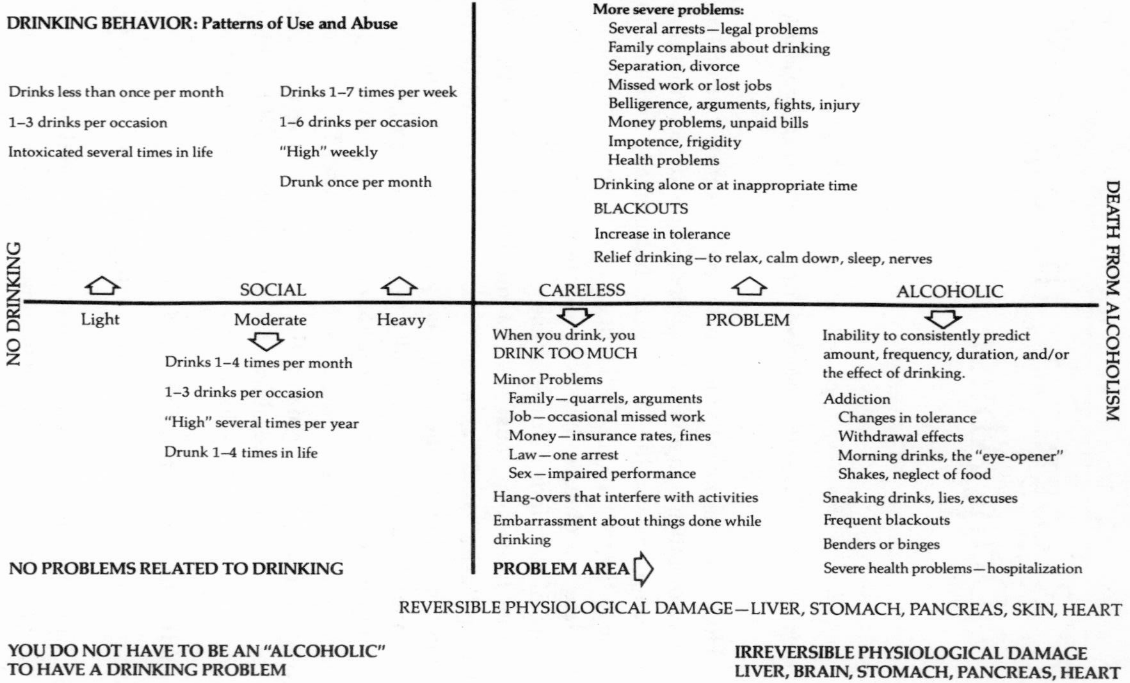

From *The Problem Drinking Continuum*, copyright 1985 Do It Now Foundation, Phoenix, Az. Used by permission.

"careless" drinkers, does not exist in real life. But as drinking becomes more frequent, heavier, and longer lasting, the problems associated with drinking build. Minor problems such as family quarrels associated with drinking can build into more severe difficulties. The family avoids discussing embarrassing incidents that occurred when the person was drinking. Further over on the problem drinking continuum is addiction and irreversible physiological damage. In short, one does not have to be alcoholic to have a drinking problem.

The same situation exists with other drugs. There are no distinct lines between light, moderate, and heavy use, or between social, careless, problem, and addictive usage. Instead, an accumulation of signs indicates that drugs have become a problem.

SIGNS THAT REVEAL DRUG ABUSE

As someone married to an addict, I'd like to know what the facts are. I don't feel like I can believe that the things he's telling me are true, because I tend not to believe him when he's talking about drugs.

A variety of physical, psychological, social, and behavioral signs may indicate that a family member has a drug problem. Although some signs may vary according to the drugs being used, many signs characterize substance abuse in general. A simple approach is to ask, "Are drugs something this person needs, either physically, psychologically, socially, or as revealed in his or her behavior?" If the answer is "yes," then a problem may be developing.

The beginning of Chapter 2 contained some questions that can reveal whether or not drug use has become a problem *for the family*. Each of the sections below begins with several questions that a family member can ask to indicate whether drug use is becoming a problem *for individuals in the family*.

PHYSICAL SIGNS OF DRUG ABUSE

1. Is the person having more medical problems?
2. Has the person been losing weight?

3. Are there more frequent upper respiratory infections, colds, runny nose, or eye infections or redness?
4. Does it take more of the drug for the person to get the desired effect?

Medical problems seem to go hand-in-hand with drug abuse. People who abuse drugs are often in poor health from neglect, poor diet, and the long-term effects of drug abuse. In an excellent book written for the general public, Sidney Cohen has summarized the medical problems that can accompany drug abuse.[1] These include loss of weight, nausea, changes in skin color, eye, nose, and throat difficulties, frequent upper respiratory infections, and heart problems.

Physical signs of drug abuse can vary according to the drug being abused. For example, the pupils of the eye are sensitive indicators of the effects of some drugs. When stimulants like amphetamines are used the pupils open up; with some depressants like opiates they are pinned. Withdrawal from either drug reverses the effect. So if a person's pupils are wide open to light it may be from using amphetamines, or it may be due to withdrawal from opiates, or a number of other possibilities.

A family member can detect whether or not tolerance is developing. By "tolerance" we mean that people need to have increasingly more of a drug to get the desired effect. People do not develop a tolerance to all drugs, but when tolerance develops it can signal the beginning of difficulties. Are they using a drug more now? Do they use faster than others? Do they continue using when others have stopped? Development of tolerance can be a problem not only because it becomes increasingly costly to use the drug (because more is needed) but also because withdrawal discomfort accompanies the development of tolerance, making it more difficult to stop.

Because the physical signs are so complicated, it is wise not to base one's conclusions about drug abuse on physical signs alone. To learn more about the effects of specific drugs, a family member may want to read some general references. In 1972 Consumers Union produced *Licit and Illicit Drugs,*[2] a readable general summary about drug abuse that remains relevant more than a decade later. The 1983 book *How Drugs Can Affect Your Life*[3] provides useful information about the physical affects of a wide range of drugs.

PSYCHOLOGICAL SIGNS OF DRUG ABUSE

1. Is the person preoccupied with drugs?
2. Has the person tried to stop but been unsuccessful?
3. Does the person feel increasingly worse about him or herself?
4. Is the person using a variety of drugs to feel "up," to relax, or just to feel normal?
5. Is the person increasingly moody, irritable, or likely to have flare-ups of temper?

The psychological problems of drug abuse are more universal, but they cannot be observed by others—only inferred. Generally, the abusers feel compelled to seek the drug. They are troubled because they cannot seem to quit. The family may notice them making more statements about lack of self-worth or ability. Sometimes they have boundless energy, other times they may seem lethargic. People with a drug problem become dependent on the drug, feeling that they need the drug to get "up," to get "down," or just to stay "normal." Their moods may swing similarly, and unpredictably, because they are related to the drive-state. Do they have the drug (in which case they are assured), do they need the drug (in which case they are uneasy), have they used it recently (in which case they may be feeling good, or guilty, or both). In short, drugs have become a central part of their thinking and emotions.

Although we can never observe someone else's internal psychological states directly, we *can* infer much about people's feelings from their behavior. Look for increased or unexplained irritability, apparent mood swings, or dependence on the drug to enjoy life.

My friend has that "feel good" syndrome . . . She's going to lose her job, but she continues to say as an excuse "I just don't feel good. I don't have a lover, I don't have a boyfriend. I need to feel good."

SOCIAL SIGNS OF DRUG ABUSE

1. Does the person have a new set of friends who are unknown to the family?
2. Does the person seem uncomfortable in social situations where drugs are not available?
3. Is the person withdrawing from family activities?
4. Is there a discrepancy between the person's known income and lifestyle?

Socially, chronic drug abuse becomes a lifestyle, and participants tend to associate mostly with other drug users. They are unlikely to integrate these friendships into their family life, unless other family members also abuse the same drugs. The family member can judge whether or not the family knows most of their friends, or if friends and family are kept away from each other.

A family can tell a lot about drug abuse from the social life of people with a drug problem, especially if they attend social events together. They may want to use drugs before going to a social event, just in case there will not be much there. They may be uneasy in social situations where drugs are not available, because they do not know how to behave with others when they're not "loaded."

Along with the change in social activities, people with drug problems may also withdraw from their families. They begin to decline invitations to family activities, or they simply do not show up. Soon the family begins to make plans apart from the person with the drug problem.

As drug abuse progresses the drugs often become a financial issue. A family member can look for a difference between income and lifestyle. On the one hand the abusers can be spending a lot of money on drugs, leaving them with little spare change—or worse, leaving the family without the necessities of living. On the other hand, as drug use advances, people often get into the business end—selling drugs or finding other illegal ways to to keep up with their addiction. This may leave them with an unexplained financial windfall one day, and apparent poverty the next. These can be clues to the family and, at later stages of drug abuse, a considerable burden:

Everything I get that is of any value, he gets rid of it. I had a lovely camera, and he got rid of that. I had a diamond ring, and that disappeared. Anything that you have that's of value—if he wants a fix, why he just steals it.

BEHAVIORAL SIGNS OF DRUG ABUSE

1. Is the person missing school or work more often?
2. Is the person less responsive to the family, seeming not to care?
3. Is the person denying, minimizing, or hiding the drug use?

Unreliability is the most telling clue. The drug abuser may be absent frequently from work; at home, family members do not expect the drug dependent people to follow through on commitments. Their unreliability gets them into trouble increasingly. If the unreliability comes in the context of wondering whether or not their drug taking is "abuse," then the answer is probably yes.

They may also be unresponsive, seeming to tune out the world. Sometimes that shows as simply not caring about things that once seemed important. Other times the unresponsiveness appears as poor appetite, accident-proneness, lack of interest in sex, or poor personal hygiene:

When he's on drugs he doesn't care, maybe he doesn't worry. . . . When they're on dope they're not worried about cleanliness or their own body. You have to fight with them to make them get in the shower. . . . I don't think he has the desire sexually for any woman. I really think the drugs take that away.

A person's drug problem can become evident in the scope of his or her denial. The close family member may notice when people with drug problems "play down" the level of drug use or deny that they have been "using" even in the face of hard facts. They become increasingly secretive. Along with denial of drug use comes changes in their general honesty about other aspects of their lives. The family should remember, during these times, that this dishonesty is not deliberately directed at the family. Instead, it is part of a general pattern in which drug users are attempting to fool everyone about their drug use, including themselves. Soon they may truly be unable to distinguish between truth and fiction in many nondrug aspects of their lives.

Finally, I confronted him. "You aren't pulling your weight in this family. You come in too late. We can't depend on you. How much of this problem is related to drugs?" But he denied everything. Later he was arrested for possession—and he still hung onto the story that he didn't use drugs.

HOW A FAMILY MEMBER CAN HELP

Once the family has assessed the problem, the issue becomes how to intervene effectively to stop a downward slide. What can be done to help directly? It will be easier to approach this issue if the family member has thought beforehand about when to bring up the subject, how to express concern, invoke consequences, handle the delicate issue of money, and build the person's ties with the drug-free world. A family member can be helpful in many ways.

TALK TO PEOPLE WHEN THEY ARE "STRAIGHT"

We do have our moments, when we talk. But they're very rare. It's, "Do I catch him before he's gotten high or after?" Which one's better, which one's worse?

When people are intoxicated, discussions can get out of hand. Communication is perilously difficult when alcoholics are intoxicated or drug abusers are "loaded." As one drug abuser said to us: "It's as if she was talking to me through a filter. Nothing important got through." Talking to people who are intoxicated is unlikely to lead to behavior change.

Communication is just as difficult when people are in withdrawal. People in withdrawal from drugs will feel anxious and may be physically ill. Despite the intentions of a family member, any conversation about drug use is likely to be met with resentment. What gets through is a sense of rejection and anger, but not a sense of caring.

When there is stress in his life there is stress in mine. I end up talking at him and we both stop listening.

The professional has an easier time than the family does in reaching the drug abusers when they are "straight." For example, Nicholas Cummings[4] will conduct an initial therapy session, but he refuses to make a second appointment until the substance abuser has found a way to "clean up." A family member, however, usually does not have the option of refusing to see drug abusers until they have stopped using drugs. Instead, the family member will need to select the right time to approach the problem, even when the drug abusers are in the middle of an addictive pattern of drug use. To reach them at all, the family member needs to talk with them when they are as close to normal functioning as possible—in the narrow band between intoxication and withdrawal.

EXPRESS PERSONAL CONCERN

It is never easy to deliver an unpleasant message. Despite the intentions of a family member, drug abusers are likely to experience confrontation about drug abuse as unpleasant. Expressing concern is one way to minimize this resistance. By saying that the family is worried about them, a family member is more likely to stay on their side. This approach works better than telling them that the family dislikes what they are doing.

Think of it as a talk with a person one is concerned about, not as a confrontation. The family member is giving honest feedback. As simply as possible, a family member can tell them what he or she is worried about and that the family member needs to understand what is going on. This can be a first chance for them to ask for help. (Chapter 5 discusses "I statements" and other communication techniques.)

People express their concern in different ways. Some are direct, others are nurturing. Either approach can be helpful, as long as the person with the drug problem understands that a family member is concerned:

When he came home I knew we had to do it together, as two people joining together, mother and son. So I said, "Are you hungry? Do whatever you need to do to relax. Then whenever you feel like talking, we're here for each other."

INVOKE CONSEQUENCES

I told my husband that he had no job, and he wanted to be with me, so I just didn't want to see him until he made something of himself or showed that he was going to do better. Until then I wouldn't advise him to come home.

I drew some definite limits: No one dealing drugs can come into the house.

Diana, I'm on your side all the way, but I've got to tell you how I feel and set some rules. I know you stole my money. Now when you're in trouble you can call me, and I'll help you. But you are not going to live in my house. I can't allow it.

The people quoted above understood the importance of putting actions behind their words. Support will go only so far. There are times when a family member must draw the line. Sometimes this is necessary to save the rest of the family. In other cases the consequences need to be enforced to give a clear message—that the drug user's behavior must change if he or she expects to keep positive ties with the family. If they are to be effective, threats must be carried out.

As is the case with reaching people when they are straight, in some ways the process of invoking consequences is easier for a professional to carry out than it is for a family member. For example, as psychologists running drug treatment programs we often discharge people from treatment when they continue to abuse drugs, even after our best efforts to help them are not working. We do this with the rationale that other people can benefit more from our treatment, and that if people are not taking treatment seriously, they are wasting both their time and ours.

Such a consequence is not so easy for a family member to invoke. The family is involved well before the professional and will continue to be involved in the person's life long after treatment has ended.

Consequences do not always have to be negative. The family can reward improvement also. Rewarding people for following through on commitments can be easier to do, less drastic, and just as important as following negative behaviors with negative consequences. In a sense "catching them at being good" is the family member's most important task. This is how the family can deliver hope, rather than discouragement.

He wanted to get help, so he came out here. I figured that if he was serious, I'd help him get into a program. So I let him live with me.

SUPPORT DOES NOT MEAN MONEY

The way it is now, drug peddlers get all my husband's money. It's owed out before he gets it. When he gets his check, he gives me some little bit for food and things for our baby, and they get the rest. He cashes his check in the morning, and he's broke in the afternoon.

When people are abusing drugs, giving them money is seldom a solution to their problems, no matter how desperately they may want it. Moreover, giving money worries the family member who gives it, and it can cause significant family hardships. In our work with families of drug abusers, perhaps the single action they most often regret is having given money to their troubled relative. Parents provide rent money to help their son, but he does not spend it on rent. They give him money to prevent him from going to jail for unpaid parking tickets, but he continues not to pay them. Assisting drug abusers *can* be helpful, and it is a fine way to show that the family cares. When the addiction has worsened, the family may think money will buy peace and quiet; but this is only temporary. The key concept to remember is that it is dangerous to give money to a person troubled by drugs—dangerous both to the drug abuser and to the family's relationship.

He used to borrow from me. "Give me $20, and I'll pay you back when I get paid." Then another $20. But when payday comes, he'll give me $10 and owe me the rest. Then the borrowing starts again. I got tired of that and I told him, "No more. You never pay me back what you owe me. No more loans. You get your money from somebody else."

BUILD FAMILY TIES WITH THE DRUG-FREE WORLD

The family *can* help the drug abuser reach for a new life where drugs are not involved. This might mean getting one's son into treatment, or one's daughter out of a chaotic living situation. Sometimes it might just mean taking them to a ballgame when they are "clean." These activities hold great promise for the family, because they both discourage drug abuse and encourage more healthy attitudes. A man takes his sister to the employment center to help her fill out job applications. A father takes his son camping. A mother drives her daughter to the drug treatment center. Each of these people is helping to combat drug abuse in a powerful way, by building family ties with the person who has a drug problem.

RECOGNIZING THE LIMITS

If the family identifies a drug problem and begins to take action, changes will begin to appear. The key concepts discussed in this chapter are that (1) a family member can recognize when drug abuse is getting out of hand and (2) the family can begin to help directly. A family member or friend of the family will realize, though, that changes will be small and slow at first, and they may not last.

The next chapter explains some of the self-help and professional treatment resources available to family members, to families as a whole, to drug abusers, and to others concerned about drug abuse. With these resources, family members can be more effective in stopping drug abuse and preventing its reappearance.

8. Treatment Alternatives

My sister got into treatment because she was just tired of it, going through all this to get money, borrowing from me when she can't pay me back. She wants to get a job and she wants to get her children back if possible. The oldest girl is in a foster home. She wanted all this, but she couldn't get it—couldn't get any of it while she was wrapped up in drugs. She was trying to make an effort, and she and her ex-husband started talking. They decided they were just tired. They wanted to change.

When is treatment needed? Earlier we discussed how to tell whether or not a drug problem exists for the family as a whole or for an individual in the family. In this chapter we look at treatments that are available.

When drug abuse is a problem, a number of treatments may help, depending on the nature of the problem, who has it, the resources available in the family and the community, and, most important, the motivation to change. This chapter summarizes self-help approaches, family treatment, and the kinds of programs aimed primarily at the individual who has a drug problem. The next chapter provides more information about how to obtain a particular kind of treatment, once a family member has decided to seek help.

SELF-HELP AS TREATMENT

A family that has recognized its drug problem has taken the first step. The family's first steps are usually taken without the involvement of a professional. In fact, it has been estimated that 85 percent of health care worldwide comes from self-help.[1] Self-help organizations can be useful to families, both in deciding what action to take and throughout the process of coping with drug abuse. They specialize in a kind of service that may be difficult for most professionals to provide—mutual caring, concrete support, and reassurance within a group of people with the same kind of problem.

GROUPS FOR FAMILIES

I was never able to talk with anyone about my daughter's problem. I can't talk with my family and wouldn't dare tell my friends. Then I came to one of those meetings, and there were people just like me. They had a problem in their family that they talked about. When I saw that, I felt like a great weight had been lifted off me.

In the last ten years parent-support programs have sprung up all over the country. They join the already existing "twelve-step" programs for families that patterned themselves after Alcoholics Anonymous—Al-Anon, Alateen, COCANON, Families Anonymous, and NarAnon.

TWELVE-STEP PROGRAMS FOR FAMILIES

WHAT ARE THEY?

These are fellowships of relatives and friends of people with the problem. They originated from the self-help program of Alcoholics Anonymous, to provide self-help for family members. Al-Anon is specifically for people concerned about an alcoholic. Alateen, a part of Al-Anon, is for teenagers who have been affected by someone's drinking. COCANON is for people whose lives have been affected by a friend or family member's cocaine abuse. Families Anonymous originally focused only on families of drug abusers, but now it includes parents whose children have other problems, such as delinquency or running away from home. NarAnon is for people whose lives have been affected by a drug abuser. There is a good deal of crossover, of people troubled both by alcohol and drugs. In groups, people join together hoping to solve their common problems by sharing experiences and increasing their knowledge and understanding of themselves and the person with the substance abuse problem. These groups are well-established, many of them available across the United States and in other countries.

WHAT PROBLEM DO THEY ATTACK?

The twelve-step programs do not attempt to change the substance abuser, but rather they exist to help the families of substance abusers. This is a key distinction between them and some other self-help groups for families.

An underlying theme is to "Let go and let God," meaning that families must recognize that they are powerless over the substance-abuse problem. They cannot change the substance abuser, but they can change their own attitudes and behaviors. Tender loving care for the substance abuser only puts off the day of reckoning. Love must be strong enough to let substance abusers work out their own solutions.

The serenity prayer reflects this credo:

> God grant me the serenity
> To accept the things I cannot change,
> Courage to change the things I can,
> And wisdom to know the difference.

Although not affiliated with any religion, the groups accept the belief in a higher power, which is reflected in their meetings and their literature.

WHO DELIVERS THE TREATMENT?

People share experiences with others who live with the same problems. Meetings are not led by professionals, but by members chosen from among the group. The organization is similar to that of Narcotics Anonymous, which is discussed later in this chapter.

HOW DOES IT WORK?

Chapters are organized locally; they vary in frequency of meeting time and other specifics; however, they share the same general way of attacking the problem. In small groups, people tell their stories and make their plans following the specific twelve steps of the organization. The twelve steps are reiterated at meetings.

Sometimes the theme of a meeting will be one of the steps, and what it means to a member, other times the group will share experiences informally, and sometimes a speaker will be invited. The twelve steps of Al-Anon are reprinted below.

THE TWELVE STEPS OF AL-ANON

1. We admitted we were powerless over alcohol—that our lives had become unmanageable.
2. Came to believe that a Power greater than ourselves could restore us to sanity.
3. Made a decision to turn our will and our lives over to the care of God *as we understood him.*
4. Made a searching and fearless moral inventory of ourselves.
5. Admitted to God, to ourselves, and to another human being the exact nature of our wrongs.
6. Were entirely ready to have God remove all these defects of character.
7. Humbly asked Him to remove our shortcomings.
8. Made a list of all persons we had harmed, and became willing to make amends to them all.
9. Made direct amends to such people wherever possible, except when to do so would injure them or others.
10. Continued to take personal inventory and when we were wrong promptly admitted it.
11. Sought through prayer and meditation to improve our conscious contact with God *as we understood him,* praying only for knowledge of his will for us and the power to carry that out.
12. Having had a spiritual awakening as the result of these Steps, we tried to carry this message to others, and to practice these principles in all our affairs.

*From the Twelve Steps, copyright © 1965, by Al-Anon Family Group Headquarters, Inc. Reprinted by permission of Al-Anon Family Group Headquarters, Inc. Adapted from the Twelve Steps of Alcoholic Anonymous with permission.

Like all of the twelve-step programs, these organizations for families have available considerable literature aimed at practical help and inspiration. Meetings are anonymous, in that no members need to reveal their identity, and meetings are run on a first-name basis. Newcomers are welcomed, whether or not the substance abuser in their lives is making efforts at recovery. In fact, membership in a twelve-step group can be an initial step in helping the substance abuser to begin recovery. There is no charge for belonging to the organizations or attending their meetings, although meetings may ask for a small donation to cover their expenses.

The next chapter includes information about how to get in touch with Al-Anon, Alateen, COCANON, Families Anonymous, and NarAnon. Generally, the twelve-step groups are so widespread that a good first step is to call your local Alcoholics Anonymous and ask if twelve-step groups for families are available in your community.

PARENT SUPPORT GROUPS

WHAT ARE THEY?

These groups consist of parents who decided to meet regularly because they found that they were not effective individually in changing the degree to which their children were exposed to and influenced by drugs. The groups aim both at individual support and community action. The concerned parents movement grew phenomenally in the early 1980s, and by 1984 there were approximately three thousand parent groups in the United States.[2] These include such groups as Toughlove, PRIDE, and local and state chapters of the National Federation of Parents for Drug-Free Youth.

WHAT PROBLEMS DO THEY ATTACK?

The groups cover a wide spectrum of activities, from increasing parent skills or family communication to influencing legislation.

Some focus more on prevention than on treatment, but all are examples of self-help.

WHO DELIVERS THE TREATMENT?

The groups rose out of lay resources; professionals were seldom involved in their development or ongoing functioning. In this way, like the twelve-step programs, these self-help groups have remained independent of professional treatment.

HOW DO THEY WORK?

Parent groups give family members the opportunity to compare notes with others in a similar situation. Some provide structured learning experiences. In addition, they can be the source of considerable information about drug abuse, and they provide windows for learning about other resources available in the community. The groups also provide a chance for families to get involved in community action aimed at preventing drug abuse—such activities as lobbying to decrease the frequency of appearance of drugs on television programs or to make drug paraphernalia less available in local stores. In short, they provide an outlet for community action. Most groups cost nothing to attend, and membership fees, when they exist, are generally quite reasonable.

The next chapter lists several national organizations with information about self-help groups. The National Federation of Parents for Drug-Free Youth (NFP) provides guidance to parent groups and represents their interests in the country's national legislative bodies. The Parent Resource Institute for Drug Education (PRIDE) has an extensive amount of educational materials available. A book by J. D. Baron[3] contains detailed advice about how to organize a parent peer group. In addition, Toughlove is explained well in a book by the same name.[4] The National Institute on Drug Abuse has published three useful documents about the parent movement, each of which provides valuable information about how to organize. *Parents, Peers, and Pot*[5] provides so much practical information that over 850,000 copies have been distributed. *Parents, Peers, and Pot II: Parents in Action*[6] documents the variety of parent groups that have been formed around the country. A third useful document is the *Manual for Working with Parents of Adolescent Drug Users,*[7] which is directed at agencies that work with adolescents. It outlines techniques for organizing and operating guided self-help groups for parents of drug-abusing young people. All are available from the National Clearinghouse for Drug Abuse Information (see Chapter 10); single copies are free.

SELF-HELP FOR DRUG ABUSERS

Families should know that self-help groups for drug abusers are accessible and can be of help. Groups are made up of people in the unique position of having "been there." The groups give both the chance to ask for help with personal problems and the opportunity to contribute to the recovery of others. The family can encourage the drug abuser to get in touch with self-help groups.

TWELVE-STEP PROGRAMS FOR DRUG ABUSERS

Narcotics Anonymous meetings have been a tremendous help to me. Usually when I come out of a meeting, my obsession with "using" has left me.

WHAT ARE THEY?

Narcotics Anonymous originated in the 1950s as a spinoff of Alcoholics Anonymous, which began in 1935. Alcoholics Anonymous (AA) is the most prevalent of the self-help organizations for substance abusers: There are at least 27,000 chapters of AA in some ninety different countries.[8] Narcotics Anonymous is less widespread, with two hundred to three hundred chapters as of the mid-1970s. At the local level, Narcotics Anonymous (NA) meetings are originated usually by AA members with a dual addiction to alcohol and drugs. These are not directed at people who have a problem only with "narcotics" (heroin, morphine, and so forth), but they are for people who have a problem with drugs in general. Over the years other drug-specific groups have been created, such as Cocaine Anonymous. The drug-specific groups have not spread as widely as NA, however, and a person with a cocaine problem would be welcomed at Narcotics Anonymous meetings.

WHAT PROBLEM DO THEY ATTACK?

Twelve-step meetings help individuals to cope with their own addiction. They emphasize the individual's responsibility for his or her own addiction. Help needs to come from within, with guidance from others in similar situations and trust in a higher power. The general goal of people in the organizations is to live clean and sober, not to reform others. Members emphasize that the program works by attraction, rather than by promotion. Members are not recruited to join the organization; however, some chapters have a hospitals and institutions committee that makes presentations at treatment centers.

WHO DELIVERS THE TREATMENT?

The programs consist entirely of people with drug problems making attempts at recovery. Like other twelve-step programs, each chapter elects a secretary who usually is responsible for arranging meetings and topics. Groups also make use of a sponsor system, in which longer-term members who have demonstrated their ability to remain abstinent may sponsor newer members. The sponsor system is characteristic of all the twelve-step programs, including those for families. One of the tenets of the twelve-step meetings is that they remain unorganized. In this respect members do not belong to a "group," but rather they attend meetings, most of which are open to new members at any time. Members are encouraged to attend as many meetings as possible.

HOW DOES IT WORK?

The groups use the twelve steps and twelve traditions of Alcoholics Anonymous (listed earlier in this chapter) adapted to fit the needs of the drug abuser. The twelve traditions provide insight into the general beliefs of the twelve-step groups as organizations. They are listed below.

THE TWELVE TRADITIONS OF NARCOTICS ANONYMOUS

1. Our common welfare should come first; personal recovery depends on NA unity.
2. For our Group purpose there is but one ultimate authority —a loving God as he may express himself in our Group conscience; our leaders are but trusted servants, they do not govern.
3. The only requirement for membership is a desire to stop using.
4. Each Group should be autonomous, except in matters affecting other Groups, or NA as a whole.
5. Each Group has but one primary purpose—to carry the message to the addict who still suffers.
6. An NA Group ought never endorse, finance, or lend the NA name to any related facility or outside enterprise, lest problems of money, property, or prestige divert us from our primary purpose.
7. Every NA Group ought to be fully self-supporting, declining outside contributions.
8. Narcotics Anonymous should remain forever nonprofessional, but our Service Centers may employ special workers.
9. NA, as such, ought never be organized; but we may create service boards or committees directly responsible to those they serve.
10. NA, as such, has no opinion on outside issues; hence, the NA name ought never be drawn into public controversy.
11. Our public relations policy is based on attraction rather than promotion; we need always maintain personal anonymity at the level of press, radio, and films.
12. Anonymity is the spiritual foundation of all our Traditions, ever reminding us to place principles before personalities.

Like other twelve-step programs, meetings usually involve talks by members who share their experiences in staying abstinent and reports by new members about how they are implementing the twelve steps, with occasional presentations by outside speakers.

By following the twelve steps, using the support available at meetings and from one's sponsor, the drug abuser creates a structured, personal program of recovery. The twelve-step programs are available without charge, and newcomers are welcomed.

Family members can encourage a drug abuser to attend these meetings, but they should keep in mind that the program's philosophy emphasizes self-determination. From this perspective families should not force a person with a drug problem to attend meetings, but rather family members should obtain help *for themselves* through COCANON, Families Anonymous, or NarAnon. Information on how to reach Alcoholics Anonymous, Cocaine Anonymous, and Narcotics Anonymous is contained in Chapter 10.

OTHER SELF-HELP GROUPS FOR DRUG ABUSERS

Beyond the twelve-step programs, few self-help groups have been established for drug abusers, and they are not available in most communities. Some self-help groups include people with drug problems, particularly people leaving the penal system, but their focus is not specifically on drug abuse. The therapeutic community concept, with its roots in self-determination, can be considered as self-help; however, in this chapter we describe therapeutic communities under treatment alternatives. Groups focusing on teenage drug abuse are another kind of self-help that may be available in a community; these groups are summarized later in this chapter under drug prevention programs.

Alumni associations of treatment programs have met with some success. The Hong Kong-based Society for the Aid and Rehabilitation of Drug Abusers (SARDA) is the best established of these groups, with a twenty-year track record.[9] A key concept in SARDA's success is "reciprocal altruism"—the drug abuser gives back to the community through community service projects. The components of SARDA include regular fellowship meetings where members share their experiences, a big-brother system (similar to the sponsor program of twelve-step programs), recreational activities, and concerned followup with members who seem to be dropping out of sight. The SARDA concept has been replicated with some success in Massachusetts, with a written guide on how to organize and run an alumni association.[10]

David Nurco and his colleagues pioneered the professional organization of self-help groups in a project in Baltimore.[11] They organized two groups, one with former narcotics addicts and another with people enrolled in methadone maintenance. Professional staff organized the groups, then attempted to phase out professional participation. The effort was successful with the group of former addicts, but less so with the people enrolled in methadone maintenance. Overall, Nurco found the concept of "giving back" to be useful. He concludes that the self-help group is an appropriate next step to help drug abusers who have worked out their addiction problems in a formal treatment program. His group has published a *Manual for Setting Up Self-Help Groups of Ex-Narcotic Addicts,*[12] which provides step-by-step organizing guidelines. Aside from these few pioneering efforts, however, self-help programs for drug abusers have not caught on in most communities. The twelve-step programs for drug abusers, however, are available in most metropolitan areas; when they are not, people with drug problems can attend meetings of Alcoholics Anonymous.

FAMILY TREATMENT

We have seen how one family member's drug abuse can cause problems for the entire family; that families suffer when coping with drug abuse; that they may foster drug abuse in the current or later generations; and that *they play a vital role in combating drug abuse.* Thus we emphasize the importance of family treatment of drug abuse.

In an excellent book for families of alcoholics, Sharon Wegscheider[13] compares the family to a mobile composed of five or six butterflies, all of different sizes, suspended by strings from several sticks. The butterflies represent the family members, and the strings and sticks the family rules. Change in one member affects the others; a powerful outside force can send everyone reeling; and after being buffeted, the family tends to return to equilibrium. If a person wants to initiate change in the family mobile, several points of leverage are available. This section discusses a number of different approaches to family treatment of drug abuse.

FAMILY THERAPY

Family therapy assumes drug abuse is part of the family system. To make lasting changes in the troubled member's drug abuse, it is necessary for the family as a whole to change. The assumption is that there are usually some underlying family problems, if for no other reason than that each person has had to make adjustments to the drug abuser's behavior. In short, if the problems of each family member are not addressed, the drug abuse is likely to return.

WHAT IS FAMILY THERAPY?

Family therapy is an approach to change in which all available family members are brought together under the leadership of a professional therapist. Family members describe their problems, and the therapist helps them toward resolution. Usually sessions take place in the office of a mental health professional or a clinic. Sessions typically last one to two hours. The length of treatment varies, with a minimum of ten sessions.

Family therapists use different models of change. Some use a *nonhistorical* model, which emphasizes the immediate family and seeks to involve all members of the household in therapy. The focus is generally on changing patterns of communication and reducing drug abuse. Consequently, these therapists will require that all family members attend the sessions. Other therapists use a *historical* model of family change, which takes into account the intergenerational history of the family and seeks to involve the extended family as part of the therapy. The emphasis is on the welfare interests of all family members affected by the problem. The focus is on improving relationships and reducing drug abuse. This model requires one or several family members to participate.

What Problems Does It Attack?

Family therapy is used for a variety of problems; for drug abuse it focuses on helping the family to change in a way that will be more healthy for the family, which usually means overcoming the drug abuse along with other problems. Some therapists focus on the drug problem and help all family members to combat it by working together. In other models the focus will be on the family generally, with drug abuse regarded as a symptom of more important underlying difficulties. In either case drug abuse is viewed as part of the family context, and participants discuss a number of family issues aimed at improving family relations.

Who Delivers the Treatment?

The therapist should be a qualified mental health professional. This is usually a psychiatrist, psychologist, social worker, or marriage and family counselor.

How Does It Work?

People in family therapy explore a number of ways to initiate change. A first step is to establish a dialogue among family members so that they can make new attempts at solving problems. If family members are too distant, they may make changes that tighten family bonds. If the family is too close, they may make changes that allow each other more autonomy. If one member is silently grief-stricken about the loss of a loved one, they may bring this out into the open so that the mourning process can be completed. If the family is disorganized, parents may be brought together to deal more effectively with the problems of the children. There is likely to be homework in the therapy—not reading materials, but completing assigned tasks aimed at improving relationships. Costs of sessions vary considerably. Most clinics and publicly supported programs will charge on the basis of a family's ability to pay.

Several aspects of family therapy can make it particularly effective with drug problems. By working together, family members pool their resources, sometimes with potent effects. The family is encouraged to expand its resources by building ties with more distant relatives. In addition, family therapy can uncover issues that have been preventing the drug abuser from making a more serious attempt at recovery. Family therapy may be particularly effective in preventing relapse to drug abuse because it concentrates on ways that the family can prepare for the drug abuser's recovery. In our work on family therapy with drug abusers, perhaps the greatest benefit families have expressed is that they get a chance to reasonably discuss issues that have been difficult to talk about in everyday life.

We talked about some things—little things like squeezing the toothpaste tube and making the bed—in a deeper way than we could ever do at home. Normally, I wouldn't want to say so much about them because it would lead to a big fight if I pushed it. Dealing with one simple thing is a lot easier than taking the whole chunk of drug abuse. We just couldn't do that at home.

PSYCHOEDUCATIONAL TRAINING

Sometimes families want to improve their situation, but they do not want family therapy. They may not be motivated to change their family, or some members will not attend, or family members may want information about drug abuse rather than therapy. In these cases a psychoeducational training program may be the treatment of choice.

What Is It?

Psychoeducation involves structured learning experiences, generally in groups attended by members of several families. A number of these training packages are available, with various goals and theoretical orientations. Parenting skills training programs, designed exclusively for parents, focus on parenting issues. Family skills training programs are offered to family units (including children), and they focus on skills associated with effective family functioning. These two brands of psychoeducation are summarized in a booklet entitled *Family Life Skills Training for Drug Abuse Prevention,* published by the National Institute on Drug Abuse.[14] Our experience has been in a third kind of training—a psychoeducational program for family members in multiple-family groups. Although the various approaches differ in goals and styles of delivery, each provides both education and a chance to explore the emotional issues that accompany living with a person who has a drug problem.

WHAT PROBLEMS DOES IT ATTACK?

Most parenting skills training programs do not focus specifically on drug abuse; rather, they are more broadly applicable to parenting issues. Parent Effectiveness Training (PET) teaches communication, problem solving, and mediation skills. Systematic Training for Effective Parenting (STEP) teaches child rearing skills. These are not specifically designed to combat drug abuse, but the skills they teach may help minimize the effects of drug abuse on the rest of the family.

Similarly, most of the family life skills training programs known to us are not specifically tied to drug abuse. They have in common, however, that they view the family as a system that can control its own destiny. Relationship Enhancement[15] teaches skills of empathy and expression. The Structured Enrichment program of L'Abate[16] provides training modules designed to meet the specific needs of a family. One program was developed specifically for families at high risk for drug abuse: The Family Effectiveness Training program designed by the Spanish Family Guidance Center of the University of Miami[17] provides drug information, along with a variety of communication and conflict resolution skills.

Our own approach to psychoeducation—aimed at family members of drug abusers—combines information about drug abuse and the family with exploration of the individual situations of family members who are sponsoring a person in drug treatment.[18]

WHO DELIVERS THE TREATMENT?

Typically, psychoeducational training programs are led by trained or certified leaders or else by trained mental health professionals. For example, in the STEP and Relationship Enhancement programs, leaders undergo extensive training in the approach and then become certified trainers. Family Effectiveness Training and our own psychoeducational groups are led by mental health professionals.

HOW DOES IT WORK?

These approaches vary considerably in format. Some are taught to many people in a classroom, others in a treatment program or the office of a professional, still others in the home. Some involve multiple-family groups, others focus on one family at a time. The psychoeducational programs draw on a variety of learning tools. Some of these involve interaction such as asking people to tell their stories, role playing, structured exercises, coaching, and practice. Most give a considerable amount of information through lectures, reading materials, or viewing film or videotapes. These programs work because they apply educational concepts to the particular situations of their participants.

Chapter 9 explains how to obtain psychoeducational training. In addition to the structured programs mentioned here, a family member could investigate the availability of psychoeducational programs at family service associations, community colleges, or as an adjunct to parent groups or local treatment centers. Some programs provide this kind of training for families of people in treatment, and parent peer groups usually are aware of the psychoeducational programs available in the community. Generally these programs are offered for a fee, which varies by type of program and locale.

DRUG ABUSE TREATMENT

The goal of this section is to give families an overview of the various treatment programs aimed primarily at the individual who has a drug problem. A person concerned about drug abuse will learn the varieties of outpatient drug-free treatment, what a detoxification clinic is, what therapeutic communities try to do, and the uses of methadone maintenance. This is a topic that relatives and friends of substance abusers usually learn through experience, rather than by a systematic presentation. The aim is to create a group of informed consumers of the things that programs offer to family members who have a drug problem.

GOALS NOT JUST TO HELP PEOPLE

The cost of drug problems is measured in lost lives, medical care and treatment for addiction, criminal activities, in people unemployed who would be working, and in people who are in prison for drug abuse. Altogether in 1981 in the United States these costs were about $16 billion.[19] Drug treatment programs have a number of different constituencies—medical, criminal, and rehabilitative. The goals of these programs are not just to help people with a drug problem, but to serve the community as well.

One goal held by programs is that people stop abusing drugs. When people are really dependent on a drug, they will do many things to get it. For example, without heroin an addict will first become shaky, then painful withdrawal symptoms build over several days to something fairly miserable. Consequently, obtaining heroin becomes the most important thing in the addicted person's life. That makes the person unreliable to everyone except the drug dealer; and that in turn makes the addicted person dangerous. One of the goals of drug programs is to get people to stop depending on street drugs, thus lessening the danger both to the drug abuser and to the community.

A second goal of most drug programs is to cut down on criminal behavior. In our heroin detoxification clinic, for example, the people who come in use about $140 a day worth of heroin. A habit of $140 a day adds up to about $52,000 a year, a sum that few drug abusers make without resorting to criminal activities. One study recently looked in detail at the lives of 243 people addicted to heroin in Baltimore.[20] In the previous ten years those 243 people had committed 473,000 crimes, or about 178 crimes per year. There is a close association between heroin addiction and criminal behavior. With other drugs the association is not so strong, but the criminal aspect can still be substantial. Consequently, one goal of drug programs is to cut down on the criminality of drug abusers.

A third goal is the one that most people usually think of— rehabilitation or recovery. We all care about that. It is important for the former drug abuser to know how to get a job, to find support in the non-drug world, and to learn how to deal with frustration without having to get "loaded."

Program goals are different from rehabilitation alone. Some programs aim at total rehabilitation of patients, others are oriented more toward stopping their drug use or cutting down on criminal behavior. Consequently, many drug programs are very tough-minded places. There is no excuse for hostility in any drug programs but a family member should know that staff in some programs can be tough.

In considering the various kinds of treatments explained below, families can keep in mind that the types of programs differ in their emphasis on rehabilitation, decreased criminality, and stopping drug use. The family can make informed choices depending on the kinds of problems being experienced by the drug abuser or the family.

OUTPATIENT DRUG-FREE TREATMENT

Outpatient drug-free programs offer counseling to drug abusers or their families. The term "outpatient drug-free" encompasses a variety of treatment programs that have little in common with each other, except that they do not use medications in treating drug abuse, and they do not offer a place to live. A youth drop-in center is an outpatient drug-free program, so is a mental health organization's counseling center. Many of the treatment techniques described under "other interventions" in this chapter are offered under the umbrella of an outpatient drug-free clinic. Altogether, outpatient drug-free treatments make up the single largest treatment modality in the United States, with some 102,000 people in treatment.

Outpatient drug-free programs can be useful for people at several stages of drug abuse. They are the most frequent first treatment for people just beginning to develop a drug problem. By talking with treatment staff, joining outpatient groups, or learning to affiliate with a better-adjusted peer group, people with a new drug problem may adjust their lifestyles so that they do not become further involved in drug abuse. These programs are also useful for the person who has completed another kind of drug treatment and wants follow-up help. For example, many therapeutic communities offer a group for people who have completed their residential stay and are facing issues of "reentry" into society. Likewise, for the drug abuser who has been through treatment and relapsed, outpatient drug-free treatment may be a way to get back on the road to recovery without needing to start over again getting medication or residential care.

DETOXIFICATION FROM DRUGS

Detoxification programs offer short-term, planned withdrawal from a drug under medical supervision. The drug may be barbiturates, heroin, or any other substance that is physically addicting. Usually these programs offer medication to alleviate withdrawal symptoms. Detoxification programs prevent the withdrawal discomfort that addicted people go through when they try to detoxify from drugs abruptly on their own ("cold turkey"). For example, in our outpatient detoxification clinic, if a person comes in with a heroin habit, we replace that heroin habit with methadone. We phase the methadone down gradually over twenty-one days of treatment (see Figure 7). If a user sticks with the treatment, at the end of twenty-one days he or she will not have withdrawal symptoms, and physically will be free of the drug. While they are in treatment we check them for any emerging medical problems like hepatitis or infections associated with using needles to take drugs.

Detoxification is a way to get rid of a physical drug habit by using supportive medication, over a time period that is short but medically reasonable. Detoxification does not cure the rest of the problems—it just takes care of the physical side.

In summary, the primary goal of detoxification is to eliminate a person's drug dependence. The second aim is to point people toward long-term treatment, where they can make other changes.

Figure 7

How Detoxification Works

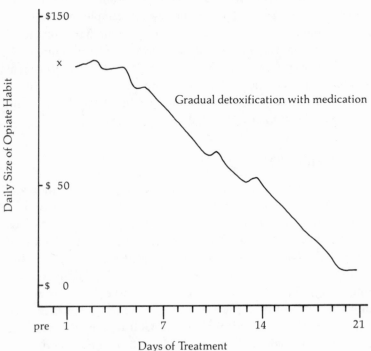

The main idea is to get people off drugs. Most detoxification is offered on an outpatient basis, although some programs provide more comprehensive inpatient care. If a family has medical insurance, inpatient detoxification may give the drug abuser a fighting chance to break the addiction cycle and make contact with followup care. On the other hand inpatient care is expensive, and the long-term outcome does not seem to be significantly different from outpatient detoxification.

Until recently, drug detoxification programs have been limited to twenty-one days of treatment. Research studies have questioned their effectiveness in helping people genuinely to give up drugs in so short a time, pointing out that clients use these programs to reduce a drug habit to a more manageable level or to provide a vacation from "hustling." The advocates of detoxification point out that keeping a drug abuser in treatment each day is a goal in itself, is cost-effective for the community, and provides the opportunity to screen for medical problems that should not be left unchecked. As of this writing federal law is extending the time limit to 180 days, and it is likely that longer-term detoxification programs will be developing with goals that give more emphasis to rehabilitation.

THERAPEUTIC COMMUNITIES

Therapeutic communities are live-in settings; well-known early programs include Synanon (the first therapeutic community), Daytop Village (the first therapeutic community for drug abusers), and Odyssey House. Today there are over three hundred therapeutic communities in the United States, and others in at least forty nations. The primary staff are non-degreed professionals, ex-addicts who have themselves been rehabilitated in a therapeutic community. One goal of these programs is to decrease drug use, which they do immediately by virtue of providing twenty-four-hour supervision. They also aim to decrease criminal behavior, and many residents go to a therapeutic community as an alternative to prison. Formal education is built into the program, most frequently helping those without a high school education to get a graduate equivalency degree.

Most important, however, therapeutic communities aim at rehabilitation. As residential programs, they make full use of the twenty-four-hour community impact to modify behavior. A resident's carelessness while washing dishes tonight can become a therapeutic issue at tomorrow morning's counseling session. Residents challenge each other to change. They go for the gut, verbally slicing back and forth in therapeutic group sessions. Residents question some of their basic assumptions about themselves. They learn to live with others. Therapeutic communities aim not only to decrease drug use or criminality, but to produce lasting personality changes.

The difficulty with therapeutic communities is that they require more commitment than other programs. A client is required to promise to stay for six months, a year, or more, and be out of contact with family for the first thirty days. Most people with a drug problem will not enter a therapeutic community. Of those who do, over 50 percent leave within a month. Nevertheless, research studies show that residents who stay at least three months make lasting changes in staying abstinent, living within the law, and finding and keeping jobs.

METHADONE MAINTENANCE

Methadone maintenance is the major drug treatment developed exclusively to treat opiate addiction. Approximately 76,000 people are in methadone maintenance treatment in the United States. The idea of maintenance is to stabilize people who have a long-term addiction, by maintaining them on a drug that replaces heroin. Figure 8 shows how this process works. A person comes in with an addiction to heroin, which the program replaces with methadone. Methadone decreases the craving for heroin because methadone itself is a narcotic. The client continues to take methadone at about the same level. Treatment continues until the person is ready to stop using methadone, which may not be for years. The main goal is to stop their abuse of heroin and get them off the streets. Rehabilitation is part of the treatment, but the main thing is to provide stability.

To understand the uses of methadone maintenance it is helpful to understand what life on heroin is like. For people with a $140-a-day habit, life is governed by heroin. They wake up at 6:00 A.M. and feel cold, the beginnings of withdrawal symptoms. They feel shaky. They pull their "works" out of the bureau drawer, and they inject heroin. They shoot themselves up well beyond any therapeutic pain-killing range of the drug, and into a range that slows their breathing and makes them feel high. Figure 9 illustrates the process.

Gradually, over the course of five to eight hours, the level of heroin in the system goes down. Meanwhile they feel fine, but as the drug level declines they begin to get anxious. They know that within a few hours they will need to find another source of heroin. They go out and hustle, they shoot up again, and they are back at the top of the chart again, in never-never land. The day is a continual roller coaster: up well beyond anything that is therapeutic, and down so that they feel withdrawal symptoms. Their days are hectic, and so are their lives.

Methadone provides stability. People get up in the morning and come to the clinic to drink their methadone dose. Unlike heroin, the effect of methadone comes on gradually—it peaks in about five hours—and then it stays with them. As Figure 10 illustrates, it also comes down gradually. Clients go to sleep at night, wake up in the morning, go to the clinic, and their last dose picks up as the previous one comes down. Instead of experiencing alternating highs and lows, they experience stability.

Of all the treatments for health-related problems, methadone maintenance is one of the most carefully studied. Research is clear that the drug itself has few detrimental side effects, that people on methadone decrease their drug use and criminality, and that their likelihood of being employed goes up while they are in treatment. Methadone maintenance is *only* for people who have had a long-term opiate addiction. To get into treatment, a person must have

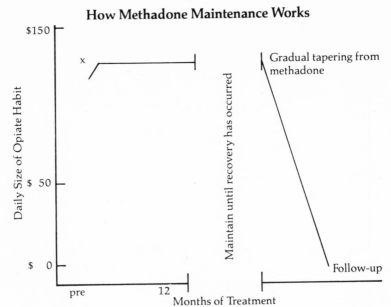

Figure 8

How Methadone Maintenance Works

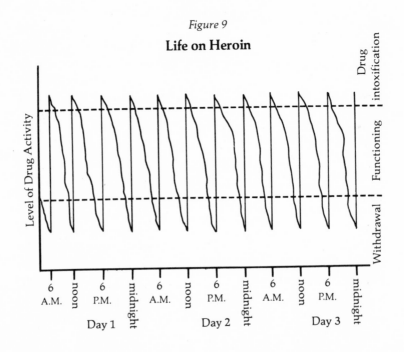

Figure 9

Life on Heroin

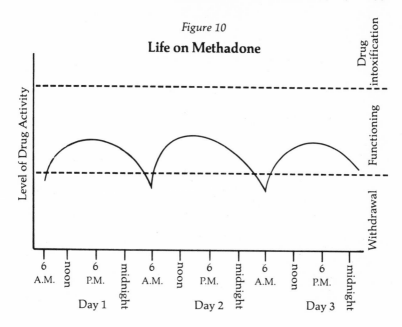

Figure 10

Life on Methadone

been using opiates for at least two years, have tried short-term detoxification programs at least twice, and nevertheless still be addicted.

The major drawback is that methadone only buys time; it is not a cure. Nothing in the chemical makeup of methadone changes a drug abuser's values, job skills, or personality. Consequently, the time on methadone can be wasted if the client does not change internally. For some people lifetime maintenance has been recommended as the only viable alternative to drug abuse, because they seem unable to make changes that would allow them to live free of opiates.

Lifetime maintenance, however, is not a goal for most people on methadone, for their families, or for treatment programs. The overwhelming majority of clients *do* eventually taper their dose and get off methadone. Aftercare can be provided in self-help programs, alumni associations, outpatient drug-free treatments, or in aftercare programs that provide a narcotic antagonist. However, if the time on maintenance was not used for personal change, then when methadone treatment ends the client will soon become addicted again.

That is why it is so important for family members to understand what is going on with people who are in methadone maintenance. A family member can help to show the client the way, help the person to get into a new group of acquaintances. When the client is not in the unstable lifestyle anymore, when the person is ready, then it is helpful to have someone who can help the client find friends, find a job, and find the will to make important changes.

OTHER TREATMENT PROGRAMS

A number of other treatment programs are available to supplement the major treatments for drug abuse. In this section we summarize several that seem to have lasting value in treatment. These include holistic treatments, relaxation and assertiveness training, narcotic antagonists, and preventive interventions.

HOLISTIC TREATMENTS

Several approaches incorporate the principles of holistic health, treating both mind and body in a planned program. Used alone or in combination with a major treatment modality, these may be helpful to a person with a drug problem.

NUTRITIONAL THERAPY

People with drug problems have poor diets. Consequently, attention to nutrition is likely to help in any attempt at recovery. Some professionals have developed structured diets specifically for drug abusers. Others advocate the use of massive doses of vitamins, or the selective use of herbs. In any case, a family can help by noticing changes that a person with a drug problem makes toward a more natural and wholesome diet.

ACUPUNCTURE

This is an ancient practice of treating disease or relieving pain by piercing parts of the body with special needles. It is used in drug abuse treatment to suppress withdrawal symptoms.[21] It may also help to fight the anxiety that goes with withdrawal, by stimulating the brain's production of endorphins, the body's natural painkillers.

RELAXATION AND ASSERTIVENESS TRAINING

Both of these approaches aim at helping the drug abuser achieve control. Relaxation training emphasizes learning techniques that, through concentration, progressively relax the muscles. Yoga and meditation have been taught to people with drug problems, as well as biofeedback and hypnotically induced relaxation. The idea is that by learning how to relax, a person can cope with the anxiety that leads to drug abuse. The results of research investigations have been equivocal.[22]

For people who are just beginning to develop a drug problem, much of the difficulty may be in not knowing how to say "no." This premise has led to including assertiveness training as a part of drug prevention and treatment programs. The theme in this kind of intervention, as in relaxation training, is for the person to attain mastery over the immediate stresses without resorting to drug use. These techniques have been used more in prevention than in treatment programs, and they show some promise for changing the attitudes of youth toward drug abuse.[23]

NARCOTIC ANTAGONIST TREATMENT

Recently a new kind of treatment has become available for people addicted to opiates: the narcotic antagonist naltrexone. An antagonist is a drug that counteracts the effects of another drug. In the case of naltrexone, it counteracts the medical effects of opiates like heroin, methadone, or morphine. When a person takes naltrexone, it occupies the opiate receptors in the brain just as effectively as a key occupies a keyhole. If the person then takes heroin, the drug will have no visible effect for approximately three days. Just as a key in a lock prevents another key from entering, so naltrexone prevents heroin from having an effect on opiate receptors.

The implications for heroin treatment programs are not yet clear; naltrexone was released by the Food and Drug Administration for distribution in late 1984, and it is just becoming available in treatment programs. The best guess is that, like the alcohol antagonist disulfiram, naltrexone will be most useful with people who have completed a treatment program and want some extra help in staying abstinent.

PREVENTION PROGRAMS FOR YOUTH

Prevention programs for youth at risk for drug abuse have special implications for treatment, in that they border on being early intervention treatment. The major preventive approach has been to teach alternatives—non-drug activities that can give pleasure, meaning, or significance to life. Thus prevention programs have emphasized a variety of growth experiences aiming at increased physical awareness (such as athletic groups), psychological and interpersonal awareness (such as growth groups), and rites of passage (such as wilderness experiences), as well as providing information about drugs and drug abuse. The impressionistic evidence is that these programs have been useful in channeling youthful energy away from drug abuse, although controlled research studies have not established their effectiveness in actually preventing teens from abusing drugs.

In the early 1980s these preventive activities increased phenomenally, principally due to grassroots interest on the part of parents. Earlier in this chapter we discussed parent support groups, which represent the self-help aspect of the parent movement. The behavior of teenagers has been the other focus of this movement. Parents have worked with educators to create school programs for youth, they have developed community services for teens, non-drug social alternatives, and programs in which teens and parents work together. Although little controlled research has established the effectiveness of these activities in preventing drug abuse, as a social movement the emphasis on prevention has had a powerful impact on social attitudes toward drug abuse and is likely to influence the development of future generations.

DECIDING TO SEEK HELP

It's still rough, but it's not as bad. At least I'm not doing it alone.

This chapter explained the nature, strengths, and drawbacks of treatments. The aim is to educate family members who will be informed consumers, so that a family member not be hesitant about seeking the treatments that are needed. The variety of treatments available were developed specifically because drug abuse is such a disabling problem. Many families are in need of help. The availability of treatment will vary depending on the resources in a community, but we encourage families to seek out the treatments that they need. A starting point is Chapter 10 of this book. Regardless of the way a family feels about admitting the need for help, sharing the problem is usually better than going it alone.

9. AIDS, Drug Abuse, and the Family

THE PROBLEM

It's just too much. I worried about my husband getting in a car wreck or getting thrown in jail because of his drug abuse. Now I find out that I have a bigger thing to worry about: He can get this deadly disease, for which there is no cure, that he might accidentally give to me or even to our children, who aren't even born yet.

At our substance abuse clinic we are seeing the beginning of a looming crisis for families in which someone has a problem with intravenous drug use. The crisis is brought about by a new disease that threatens our clients and their families: AIDS.

Acquired Immunodeficiency Syndrome, AIDS, is a treacherous disease caused by an unusual virus that breaks down the body's immune system. AIDS appears to be fatal in almost every case: Nearly all patients have died within five years after diagnosis. AIDS is increasing in overall incidence. As of this writing the number of cases is doubling every thirteen months, and more than twenty-five thousand people have been diagnosed in the United States. Many times more have been infected with the AIDS virus but have not yet developed AIDS.

Several groups are particularly at risk of acquiring AIDS: About 95 percent of the cases have been among homosexual or bisexual men, intravenous drug abusers, hemophiliacs, or the sexual partners of people in those risk groups. Seventeen percent of the known AIDS cases have been with people in the intravenous drug-abuse risk group, and at least 8 percent more of the cases have been both homosexual or bisexual male drug abusers. The AIDS virus is passed by sharing body fluids—for example, through sexual contact or using needles that carry the blood of someone already infected. In short, AIDS is a vital issue for drug abusers and their families.

WHAT IS AIDS?

Acquired Immunodeficiency Syndrome is a recent development, about which we have more questions than answers. It was not identified as a syndrome until approximately 1982, although cases have been documented retrospectively as early as 1977. AIDS breaks down the body's immune system, leaving the body vulnerable to a variety of infections and cancers that it would usually fight off. The cause of AIDS is a virus that changes the structure of the cells it attacks.

AIDS is diagnosed by the presence of unusual infections or cancers. The most common illness associated with AIDS is pneumocystis carinii pneumonia, a lung infection caused by a parasite that in most individuals is destroyed by immune cells. The second commonest illness is Kaposi's sarcoma, a skin cancer that can spread to internal organs. Other less common illnesses include fungal infections and rare cancers. AIDS has no cure as yet, nor is there a vaccine that can prevent a person from getting it. The key to preventing the transmission of AIDS is to understand how it is spread.

HOW AIDS IS TRANSMITTED

Infected body fluids spread the AIDS virus. The AIDS virus can be transmitted by sexual contact in the same way as other sexually transmitted diseases. It is spread through blood-to-blood contact in intravenous drug abusers, particularly by sharing hypodermic needles. In addition, a pregnant woman who is infected with the virus can transmit it to her child in the uterus, at the time of birth, or by nursing. In the first few years of the AIDS outbreak there were many cases of people who acquired AIDS from transfusions of blood that came from infected donors. At this time screening all blood donors for infection and discarding infected blood dona-tion, has greatly reduced the likelihood of such transmission. Although many different body fluids have been found to contain the virus (saliva, sweat, and tears), the evidence to date is that semen and blood are the two main body fluids involved in *spreading* AIDS.

BEING INFECTED DOES NOT MEAN HAVING AIDS

Many people have been infected with the virus but have not developed AIDS. The long-term effects of infection for this group are unknown, but it is known that *they can transmit the virus to others.*

A smaller group of people infected with the AIDS virus go on to develop what is called an AIDS-related complex (ARC). They develop symptoms such as swollen glands, persistent diarrhea, or unusual fungus infections. These problems seem to be due to a poorly functioning immune system, but the problems do not qualify for a full diagnosis of AIDS.

Still another group of people infected with the AIDS virus go on to develop the full syndrome of AIDS, indicated by pneumocystis carinii pneumonia, Kaposi's sarcoma, or other specific life-threatening infections or cancers that do not normally occur in healthy people. Published estimates of the number of virus-infected individuals who subsequently develop AIDS range from 0–5 percent per year. It takes anywhere from a few months to several years or more after infection for these diseases to develop. Scientists cannot be more precise because discovery of the disease is too recent: Studies will need to follow people's medical histories much longer to know what percent of people infected with the virus will eventually develop AIDS.

THE TEST FOR AIDS ANTIBODIES

When people have been infected by the AIDS virus their bodies produce AIDS antibodies, which try to fight the virus. A blood test has been developed to detect the presence of AIDS antibodies. The test is available in many communities. It is *not* a test for AIDS, but it *does* show whether or not a person has been infected with the virus that causes AIDS.

The test is controversial, because infection does not always lead to disease. Many people are concerned that they might face insurance or employment discrimination if the results of their tests were revealed. Some professionals point out that, no matter what the results, the person should do the same things to stay healthy, and in that sense the test only raises a person's anxiety. Further, no test is completely reliable, so the testing must be be done carefully and using the right methods.

On the other hand, there is a demand for the test. Some people want to know whether or not they may have been exposed to the virus and may be infectious. Couples in high-risk groups take the test to see if it is safe to have children or if they are worried about the possibility of one partner infecting the other.

AIDS SYMPTOMS

People cannot diagnose AIDS themselves—most of the initial symptoms of AIDS are nonspecific and similar to the symptoms of simple colds, bronchitis, or stomach flu. In AIDS, however, these symptoms continue or keep recurring. In a person with AIDS, the symptoms indicate that the immune system has been damaged. The general symptoms include:

- unexplained, persistent fatigue
- unexplained, persistent fever, or drenching night sweats
- unexpected weight loss of greater than ten pounds
- swollen glands (lymph nodes) unexplained by other illness and lasting longer than two weeks
- creamy white patches on the tongue or mouth
- persistent diarrhea
- persistent, frequent dry cough (not from smoking or common respiratory infection), or shortness of breath or difficulty breathing
- pink or purple painless skin blotches that don't go away and do not pale when pressed (these lesions can be due to Kaposi's sarcoma and are *not* common in drug abusers with AIDS).

If these symptoms or combinations of symptoms occur, and if there is a possibility of exposure to AIDS, the person should seek medical attention, using the information contained in the chapter on where to get help, or the toll-free numbers listed at the end of this chapter.

THE AIDS-DRUG ABUSE CONNECTION

A family member who wants to be helpful should not only understand AIDS but know how it is connected to drug abuse. Barbara Faltz and Scott Madover have pointed out six ways in which substance abuse is related to the development of AIDS— needle sharing, sexual transmission, transmission to infants, immune system damage, increased risk of exposure, and interference with treatment.[1] With this information, a family member will know both the risks and how to break the transmission cycle.

NEEDLE SHARING

The primary way that drug users transmit the AIDS virus appears to be by sharing hypodermic needles, syringes, and paraphernalia used to inject drugs. By sharing these instruments it is easy for some of the infected blood of one drug user to get injected into the body of another drug user who uses the needle next. Neither one needs to have any symptoms at the time for the infection to take place.

Not every drug user shares needles, but needle-sharing is a common practice.[2] In our heroin detoxification clinic at least half the clients admit to sharing a needle or using the needle of another person in the month before entering treatment. Sharing needles with a "running partner" demonstrates trust; when people are in withdrawal they do not pay much attention to hygienic practices; in some areas there are "shooting galleries" (places where drug abusers gather to inject drugs) that have needles available to rent. These situations provide fertile ground for the AIDS virus to spread among people who inject drugs.

TRANSMISSION TO SEXUAL PARTNERS

A second connection of substance abuse with AIDS is the transmission of the virus by an infected drug user to his or her sexual partner. Only about 1 percent of the people with AIDS in the United States have acquired it from heterosexual transmission: Of the first 154 such cases, 88 percent were women who acquired it from a man.[3] A number of these were the spouses of intravenous drug abusers. Approximately 12 percent of the women with AIDS probably acquired it from sexual contact with a man who had been exposed to the AIDS virus. Apparently AIDS may be transmitted in semen entering the vagina, rectum, or mouth.

Although the number of people who have acquired AIDS in this way is still small, this risk is a vital issue for the spouses of people who use intravenous drugs and is discussed further below.

TRANSMISSION TO INFANTS

Women who are carrying the AIDS virus can transmit it to their infants, either before or during birth. Approximately half of the cases of pediatric AIDS are in children born to mothers who used intravenous drugs, and ten percent are in mothers who either had AIDS or were sexual partners of men with AIDS or at risk for AIDS. These infants developed AIDS on the average about four months after birth; half of infants carrying the AIDS virus will be diagnosed as having AIDS by their first birthday.[4]

DAMAGE TO THE IMMUNE SYSTEM

Substance abuse is a well-known producer of health problems. Alcohol abuse is linked with a variety of physical problems, as is abuse of amphetamines, and opiates. In recent years there has been some evidence that marijuana may lower the body's ability to fight infection. Some researchers believe that the use of volatile nitrites (commonly called "poppers") may be a factor in development of

AIDS. At a minimum, substance abuse weakens the immune system, making intravenous drug abusers vulnerable to a variety of diseases, and it may make a person even more vulnerable to AIDS.

INCREASED RISK OF EXPOSURE

People who are under the influence of drugs often have impaired judgment which makes them more likely to take risks. For example, the drug user who is intoxicated may be more likely to share the needle of another, or to not use a condom during sex, even though he knows he is at high risk for having the AIDS virus. Studies of gay men reveal a significant link between continued substance abuse and continued sexual activities that are high risk for getting or giving AIDS. It is likely that this link will be present in studies of heterosexual drug users as well.

INTERFERENCE WITH TREATMENT

People who abuse drugs are not likely to reliably comply with instructions of their medical doctor, even when the treatment is for a disease as life-threatening as AIDS. In addition, the toxic effects of alcohol or drugs on the body can diminish the effectiveness of treatment for AIDS or AIDS-related complex.

IMPLICATIONS FOR THE FAMILY

Several family members of intravenous drug abusers should consider themselves as members of groups at high risk for acquiring AIDS. We think it is wise for them to change whatever activities put them at risk for acquiring (or spreading) the AIDS virus. These changes are significant ones that may upset the normal way of doing things, just as the threat of AIDS has changed norms in the other major risk group, homosexual and bisexual men. Nevertheless, we believe that family members should be informed early in the epidemic, so that they can act to minimize its impact. The general principle in each recommendation is to decrease risk by not sharing body fluids.

The family member who uses intravenous drugs should add AIDS to the list of risks of continued drug use. From a risk-management viewpoint, it is best to stop using drugs; such an action would effectively take the person out of the group at high risk for getting AIDS. Treatment and self-help programs are available, as explained in an earlier chapter of this book. Decreasingly effective alternatives are: (1) to stop taking drugs intravenously; or (2) (less effective and higher risk) to not use the needles of others; or (3) (even higher risk) to clean the needles of others before using them. For drug users who fear they may be infected, the same principle applies: Do not share body fluids. Do not share needles with others; use a condom to avoid sharing body fluids during sexual relations. Consider taking the AIDS antibody test if knowledge of the test results will help to determine whether or not to act differently.

The sexual partner of a person who uses intravenous drugs faces a difficult situation, as illustrated by the quotation that began this chapter. It hardly seems fair, after all the difficulties that a family member endures, that AIDS can multiply the levels of concern with not only fear for the drug abuser, but fear for oneself and one's yet-to-be-born children. However, that is the situation. At a minimum, the sexual partner of a drug abuser will be well-advised to avoid sexual relations that involve sharing of body fluids. A woman who is planning to become pregnant may strongly consider being confidentially or anonymously tested for the AIDS virus. Testing can be offered through private physicians, hospitals, or through clinics that may be available in the community. It may also be prudent for women with multiple sexual partners in areas with high incidence of AIDS to consider themselves at risk.

For couples where one or both use intravenous drugs, having children seems to be a risky prospect. A couple that is considering having children may be wise to postpone pregnancy until more is known about the specific risks of AIDS transmission during the birth process. At the present time no one knows how a virus-infected woman can prevent giving the AIDS virus to her children during the birth process. The level of risk faced by the infant is very high if mother, father, or both have been exposed to AIDS. We do not know how to prevent these children from developing AIDS after birth.

Other family members can have important roles in giving information about AIDS to the people most at risk. They can clip newspaper articles, listen to the radio, and open discussion with the family member who abuses drugs or that person's sexual partner. Earlier in this book we presented several specific ways to talk about difficult issues and begin to take action; those techniques may be helpful to the family member who wants to discuss AIDS with a person at high risk. To slow the spread of AIDS it is crucial to get the information out as quickly and through as many channels as possible.

For all family members these issues are difficult. Knowledge about AIDS is developing at a rapid pace, and recommendations will change as more becomes known. Treatments may become more effective, preventive actions more feasible. We recommend that family members pay attention to the news about AIDS, and seek out opportunities to receive information. Until the time that a cure or a vaccine is available, however, it seems wise for family members to take the conservative approach, and avoid getting exposed to a situation from which there is no pleasant outcome.

FREQUENTLY ASKED QUESTIONS ABOUT AIDS AND DRUGS

HOW MANY DRUG USERS HAVE BEEN EXPOSED TO THE AIDS VIRUS?

No one knows, but the geographical areas differ widely. In New York, as of this writing, at least 50 percent of intravenous drug abusers test positive for the AIDS virus[5]; in San Francisco in 1985 and in New Haven in 1982 the rate was closer to 10 percent.[6] In New Jersey, the communities closer to New York City have much higher rates of AIDS than those in the southern part of the state. As we write this, in many communities none of the drug abusers have yet been exposed to the AIDS virus. However, AIDS is expanding in epidemic proportions: Cases have occurred in all fifty of the United States. People who live in relatively isolated communities will be affected eventually. For the family member, the wise course of action is to minimize the possibility of risking exposure to the virus.

IS A TEST FOR AIDS AVAILABLE?

Not exactly. A blood test can detect the presence of AIDS antibodies, which indicates that a person has been exposed to the virus. As far as we know, however, most people who have been exposed to the virus do not get AIDS. The diagnosis of AIDS is made by a physician, based on physical examination and laboratory tests.

HOW RISKY IS IT TO LIVE WITH SOMEONE WHO IS INFECTED?

The AIDS virus is not known to be airborne, nor transmitted through coughing, sneezing, food, shared silverware, and so forth. A study of household members of 100 people with AIDS or ARC showed no transmission of the AIDS virus through such everyday contact[7]. There are no known cases of anyone getting AIDS from kissing. The virus is known to be spread through sexual or blood-to-blood contact. The risks are in sharing body fluids through such activities as sexual relations or sharing needles in drug use. For these reasons, risk-reduction guidelines stress that people should not share body fluids and recommend that people use a condom during sexual intercourse. If a person is considering living with someone who is at high risk, it is wise to seek additional information, which can be obtained from the resources suggested later in the chapter.

DOES TREATMENT HELP?

First, there is no cure for AIDS; however, there are effective treatments for the infections and cancers that go with it, and these treatments can prolong a person's life. Drug abusers tend to delay being diagnosed and delay getting treatment. The average length of time between a drug abuser's diagnosis and subsequent death is only ten months.

Treatment for drug abuse will reduce the likelihood of exposure to the AIDS virus to the extent that it helps a person to stop using drugs, lead a more healthy lifestyle, and cut down on needle sharing and other behaviors at high risk for getting AIDS. Drug abuse treatment is one way to get information to those at risk and to help them to minimize their exposure to AIDS. Further, evidence suggests that repeated exposure to the virus increases the risk of developing AIDS. Just because a person has been exposed to the virus does not mean that he or she should give up hope. Instead, such people should make every effort to live more healthy lives. Some authorities have recommended that drug treatment programs be expanded during the AIDS crisis.[8]

HOW CAN I GET MORE INFORMATION?

Two toll-free telephone hotlines have been established, which are answered twenty-four hours a day. Dialing (800) 342–AIDS will get the toll-free AIDS information line operated by the U.S. Department of Public Health's Centers for Disease Control. The line has a four-minute audio tape giving information about AIDS, and a telephone number that can be called for further information.

The National AIDS 800 Hotline—(800) 221–7044—is answered by a trained counselor twenty-four hours a day. The hotline is operated by the Fund for Human Dignity and can make referrals to treatment resources in local communities.

In San Francisco the AIDS Foundation has developed numerous written materials, many of which cover the topic of drug abuse and AIDS. A catalog is available from the San Francisco AIDS Foundation, 333 Valencia Street, Fourth Floor, San Francisco, CA 94103.

AIDS presents significant problems for intravenous drug abusers and their families. People who use intravenous drugs make up 17 to 25 percent of the AIDS cases. For the family member, a realistic worry is that intravenous drug users in the family may acquire the AIDS virus, either now or as the virus spreads through communities. Several specific suggestions can help to reduce the risk.

AIDS does not change the central theme of this book: Family members can be of tremendous value in helping people to overcome drug problems. A family member can seek information about AIDS and drug abuse, can talk about the problem from a personal viewpoint, can seek the consultation of self-help and treatment programs, and can develop problem-solving skills without allowing the difficulties of the drug abuser to overwhelm family life.

What AIDS adds is yet one more deadly threat of continued drug abuse. The responsibility for quitting, however, must ultimately be that of people with drug problems and not that of their families. Family members can help in a hundred ways, but no one can make the changes *for* the drug abuser. For the family member, the proper course of action is to do what is possible to help people with drug problems understand the risks and consequences of acquiring AIDS, but at the same time do what is needed to protect oneself and other family members from the threat.

10. Where to Get Help or Information

HOW TO USE THIS CHAPTER

This chapter tells how to get the help or information that a family member may need. Like the chapter on treatment alternatives, it contains sections on self-help, family treatment, and drug treatment. Within sections, programs are listed in alphabetical order. A reader's particular needs will determine what part of the chapter to use.

To reach the resource groups mentioned, first look them up in the telephone book to see if they are available locally. If they are not listed, a telephone call to your county's drug program administrator may uncover local resources. The county drug program administrator will be listed in the government section at the front of the telephone book. (See Reaching Local Treatment Programs in this chapter.) The chapter closes with sources of general information and further reading.

SELF-HELP ORGANIZATIONS

SELF-HELP FOR FAMILIES WITH A DRUG PROBLEM

Self-help Groups for Families

Al-Anon
Alateen
Al-Anon Family Group Headquarters
P.O. Box 182
Madison Square Station
New York, NY 10159–0182

Al-Anon is for families and friends of someone with an alcohol problem. Alateen is for teenagers who are affected by the alcoholism of a family member. These are widely available self-help organizations.

COCANON Family Groups
Box 3969
Hollywood, CA 90028
(213) 859–2206

COCANON Family Groups are for families and friends of someone with a cocaine problem. Chapters exist in California, Arizona, Connecticut, Oregon, Washington, and New York. This is a growing organization.

Families Anonymous
Box 528
Van Nuys, CA 91408

Originally for families with a drug-abusing child, this group has broadened its approach to include other childhood difficulties and spouses of people with drug problems. Meetings are available in thirty-eight states and several other countries. A useful set of readings is available from Families Anonymous.

Naranon
350 West 5th Street, Suite 207
San Pedro, CA 90731

Naranon is for families and friends of someone with a drug problem. This is a widely available self-help organization.

TOUGHLOVE®
P.O. Box 1069
Doylestown, PA 18901

TOUGHLOVE emphasizes local support groups, with a philosophy of community organization and support for parents troubledby teenage behavior.

NATIONAL ORGANIZATIONS OF PARENT GROUPS

National Federation of Parents for Drug-Free Youth (NFP)
8730 Georgia Avenue, Suite 200
Silver Spring, MD 20910
(800) 554-KIDS

NFP provides information about starting parent groups, networking among groups, and drug paraphernalia issues. An NFP starter kit is available for a small fee.

Parent Resource Institute for Drug Education (PRIDE)®
100 Edgewood Avenue, Suite 1002
Atlanta, GA 30303
(800) 241-9746

PRIDE is an information and resource center providing free materials and referral assistance. PRIDE publishes a quarterly newsletter and a drug survey available for use in schools. An annual conference is held each Spring. Send for free information or call for recorded messages each evening.

INFORMATION ABOUT FAMILY GENEALOGY

For information on local and state genealogical organizations, consult the telephone directory. Below are a number of national organizations that are useful genealogical resources.

American Association for State and Local History
1400 Eight Avenue South
Nashville, TN 37203

This national organization has available national directories of genealogical and historical societies. Its *Directory of Genealogical Societies in the USA and Canada* was edited by M. K. Meyer; its *Directory of Historical Societies and Agencies in the USA and Canada* was edited by D. McDonald.

Genealogical Society
50 East North Temple
Salt Lake City, UT 84150

This society is supported by the Mormon Church. It claims the largest genealogical library in the world, with 640 branches. This society has a packet of information that includes research papers, accredited genealogical researchers, a list of branch libraries, and general information of an introductory nature for the beginning genealogist.

Library of Congress
First Street and Independence Avenue
Washington, D.C. 20540

Anyone may write to the Genealogy Section of the Library of Congress directly for information. The library has a catalog titled "Genealogies in the Library of Congress." Included are the genealogies of families from the United States and Canada, but also from England, France, Germany, Spain, Italy, Australia, Portugal, Poland, as well as from a number of Latin American and Asian countries. Large public libraries have a copy of this catalog.

National Archives and Records Service
NNC
Washington, D.C. 20408

The Archives has a summary of genealogical records that may be found in its *Guide to Genealogical Records in the National Archives,* edited by W. Linder and J. D. Walker.

National Genealogical Society
4527 17th Street North
Arlington, VA 22207–2363

This organization has information available on how to conduct genealogy research. It holds a national conference each year and has a large library.

SELF-HELP PROGRAMS FOR DRUG ABUSERS

Cocaine Anonymous
6125 Washington Boulevard
Los Angeles, CA 90230

Cocaine Anonymous is a self-help organization for people who are cocaine abusers. The number of chapters is growing.

Narcotics Anonymous World Service Office
Box 9999
Van Nuys, CA 91409
(818) 780-3951

Narcotics Anonymous is the most widespread of self-help programs for people with a drug problem, and it is *not* just for people who abuse "narcotics" but for other drug problems as well.

Alcoholics Anonymous® World Services
Box 459
Grand Central Station
New York, NY 10163

If Cocaine Anonymous or Narcotics Anonymous is unavailable in a community, there will probably be at least one chapter of Alcoholics Anonymous. AA has developed a voluminous set of publications for people affected by an alcohol problem.

FAMILY TREATMENT

FAMILY THERAPY

Family therapy is one of the core services available from mental health professionals, and it can be obtained from both private practitioners and mental health clinics. In contacting professionals for family services, inquire about their experience with substance abuse *and* family treatment. Many family therapists have little or no experience with substance abuse, and many substance abuse professionals have little or no experience in the treatment of families. We believe it is important to have experience in both family therapy and substance abuse. Below are some organizations that provide referrals.

American Association of Marital and Family Therapy
1717 K Street N.W. Suite 407
Washington, D.C. 20006

AAMFT is a national organization of child, marriage, and family counselors. The organization has independent chapters at the statewide level. AAMFT has available referral lists of licensed professionals affiliated with the organization.

American Family Therapy Association
1815 H Street, N.W. Suite 1000
Washington, D.C. 20006

AFTA is a national organization of teachers, researchers, theoreticians, and clinicians in family therapy. The organization publishes a directory that may be obtained by writing to the central office.

Family Service Association of America
44 East 23rd Street
New York, NY 10010
(212) 674-6100

There are over 270 local Family Service Agencies in North America, providing access to family therapy and also directly providing family life education programs.

PSYCHOEDUCATIONAL TRAINING FOR FAMILIES

To learn about local programs, we suggest contacting the local Family Service Association if there is one available in the community (see above). The resources below are listed because we know them to be well-established training programs.

Bicultural Effectiveness Training
Spanish Family Guidance Center and
University of Miami Drug Abuse Programs
University of Miami School of Medicine
1425 N.W. 10th Avenue
3rd Floor
Miami, FL 33136

The Spansih Family Guidance center conducts research, training and services in teaching parenting skills and family communication; prevention and treatment of adolescent behavior problems, including drug abuse; family and marital conflicts; depression in the elderly.

Parent Effectiveness Training (P.E.T.)®
531 Stevens Avenue
Solano Beach, CA 92075

PET teaches communication skills, problem solving, and conflicting resolution skills to parents in an eight-session course. Write for addresses of P.E.T. instructors in your state.

Relationship Enhancement
Dr. Bernard Guerney
Individual and Family Consultation Center
Catherine Beecher House
Pennsylvania State University
University Park, PA 16802

Relationship Enhancement teaches skills of empathy, expression, and facilitation to individual families.

Structured Enrichment
Dr. Luciano L'Abate
Department of Psychology
Georgia State University
University Plaza
Atlanta, GA 30303

Structured Enrichment has several skill-development programs, offered to individual families depending on their specific needs.

Systematic Training for Effective Parenting (S.T.E.P.)
American Guidance Service, Inc.
Circle Pines, MN 55014

American Guidance Service, Inc. provides information about STEP. A sixteen to twenty-four hour training program for groups of eight to fifteen, STEP teaches skills in family interaction and communication.

DRUG ABUSE TREATMENT

REACHING LOCAL TREATMENT PROGRAMS

The telephone book is the quickest way to learn what is available. In most communities the phone book begins with a listing of government agencies and offices, including both city/town and county departments. Look under "drug abuse," "health," "alcoholism," or "mental health." Call to find out about resources. Another option is the yellow pages, which may have listings under those categories. If the telephone book does not have a "government" listing in front, look up county offices under the name of the county in which the family resides. Chapter 8 explains the kinds of treatment alternatives that may be available.

REACHING STATE RESOURCES

Every state and territory has an agency that is responsible for the treatment and prevention of drug abuse and alcoholism. Some states publish a directory of drug treatment programs, which is available free or for a small fee. To find the address and telephone number of the state agency, one can contact the state capitol, or write or phone to the following:

National Association of State Alcohol and
Drug Abuse Directors
444 North Capitol Street, N.W.
Suite 530
Washington, D.C. 20001
(202) 783–6868

REACHING NATIONAL RESOURCES

The federal government sponsors two offices that may be useful to family members. Each of these has knowledgeable people who can give advice about federal programs, and each has written materials available to the public.

Drug Enforcement Administration (DEA)
Public Affairs Office
1405 I Street, N.W.
Washington, D.C. 20537
(202) 633-1469

The DEA has information on the Federal Narcotics and Dangerous Drug Laws, and it has its own public information and prevention program.

National Institute on Drug Abuse
5600 Fishers Lane
Rockville, MD 20857

The federal government organizes its drug abuse treatment, research, prevention, and policy-making under the National Institute on Drug Abuse. Consequently, this organization has much information that may be helpful to families.

GENERAL INFORMATION ABOUT DRUG ABUSE

ORGANIZATIONS WITH RESOURCE MATERIALS

Readers who want more information about drug problems in general can get help by contacting these organizations.

American Council for Drug Education
5820 Hubbard Drive
Rockville, MD 20852

This private, nonprofit organization is dedicated to informing the American public about health hazards associated with the use of marijuana and other drugs. It has a variety of written materials available about the effects of marijuana and cocaine, including scientific monographs, and will provide a free catalog on request.

National Clearinghouse for Drug Abuse Information
Room 10A–56 Parklawn Building
Rockville, MD 20857

This is the distribution center for government publications about drug abuse, including all of the publications of the National Institute on Drug Abuse. These books, articles, posters, and pamphlets have accurate information that is updated continuously. Single copies of most will be sent free of charge. A catalog of publications can be obtained from the clearinghouse.

National Self-Help Clearinghouse
33 West 42nd Street
New York, NY 10036

The clearinghouse has available a directory of mutual self-help groups.

PYRAMID Project
Suite 805
7101 Wisconsin Avenue
Bethesda, MD 20814

PYRAMID, a project of the Pacific Institute for Research and Evaluation, provides technical assistance and information to drug abuse and alcohol prevention programs nationally. PYRAMID is sponsored by the National Institute on Drug Abuse.

MARKETERS OF DRUG ABUSE LITERATURE

It may be worthwhile to write to these to get on their mailing lists for publications. Each regularly updates its collection of educational materials about drug abuse.

D.I.N. Publications
Do It Now Foundation
Box 5115
Phoenix, AZ 85010

D.I.N. publishes a large number of pamphlets, booklets, and posters about drugs and drug abuse issues.

Hazelden Foundation
Box 11
Center City, MN 55012
(612) 257–4010

Hazelden publishes an annual catalog that is a comprehensive collection of materials from its own publishing house and selections from other publishers, including Alcoholics Anonymous. It includes not only pamphlets and books, but also films, video and audio tapes, posters, and more. Hazelden is one of the leading treatment organizations for alcoholism, but many of its materials are aimed at drug abuse.

Health Communications, Inc.
2119–A Hollywood Boulevard
Hollywood, FL 33020

Health Communications markets its own periodicals, pamphlets, films, tapes, conferences, and books, and selected books by other publishers and Al-Anon. One journal available from here is *Focus on Family and Chemical Dependency,* a magazine for families that have been affected by alcoholism or drug abuse.

Selected Further Reading

Alberti, R. E. and M. L. Emmons. *Your Perfect Right: A Guide to Assertive Training* (4th ed.). San Luis Obispo, CA: Impact Publishers, 1982.

Allen, W. A., N. L. Piccone, and C. D'Amanda. *How Drugs Can Affect Your Life.* Springfield, IL: Charles C. Thomas, 1983.

Baron, J. D. *Kids and Drugs: A Parent's Handbook of Drug Abuse Prevention and Treatment.* New York: GD/Perigee Books, 1981.

Brecher, E. M. *Licit and Illicit Drugs.* Boston: Little, Brown, 1972.

Boszormenyi-Nagy, I. and G. Spark. *Invisible Loyalties: Reciprocity in Intergenerational Family Therapy.* New York: Brunner/Mazel, 1984.

Bower, S. A. and G. H. Bower. *Asserting Yourself: A Practical Guide for Positive Self-change.* Reading, MA: Addison-Wesley, 1976.

Carter, E. and M. McGoldrick. *The Family Life Cycle: A Conceptual Framework for Family Therapy.* New York: Gardner Press, 1980.

Cerny, J. and A. Eakle. *Ancestry's Guide to Research.* Salt Lake City, UT: Ancestry Press, 1984.

Cohen, S. *The Substance Abuse Problems.* New York: Haworth Press, 1981.

Darten, D. A. *Quitting: Knowing When to Leave.* New York: Walker and Company, 1980.

DuPont, R. L., Jr. *Getting Tough on Gateway Drugs.* Washington, D.C.: American Psychiatric Press, 1984.

Gordon, B. *I'm Dancing as Fast as I Can.* New York: Harper & Row, 1979.

Kaufman, E. *Substance Abuse and Family Therapy.* New York: Grune & Stratton, 1985.

Levy, S. J. *Managing the "Drugs" in Your Life: A Personal and Family Guide to the Responsible Use of Drugs, Alcohol, Medicine.* New York: McGraw-Hill, 1983.

Manatt, M. *Parents, Peers, and Pot.* (DHHS Pub. No. (ADM) 81–812). Washington, D.C.: U.S. Government Printing Office, 1979.

Manatt, M. *Parents, Peers, and Pot II: Parents in Action.* (DHHS Pub. No. (ADM) 83–1290). Washington, D.C.: U.S. Government Printing Office, 1983.

McGoldrick, M. and R. Gerson. *Genograms in Family Assessment.* New York: Norton, 1985.

Nurco, D. N. and N. Wegner. *Manual for Working with Parents of Adolescent*

Drug Users. (DHHS Pub. No. (ADM) 83–1209). Washington, D.C.: U.S. Government Printing Office, 1982.

Rose, M., R. Battjes, and C. Leukfeld. *Family Life Skills Training for Drug Abuse Prevention.* (DHHS Pub. No. (ADM) 84–1340). Washington, D.C.: U.S. Government Printing Office, 1984.

Smith, M. J. *When I Say No I Feel Guilty: How to Cope—Using the Skills of Systematic Assertive Therapy.* New York: Dial Press, 1975.

Stanton, M. D., T. C. Todd, and Associates. *The Family Therapy of Drug Abuse and Addiction.* New York: Guilford Press, 1982.

Watzlawick, P., J. Weakland, and R. Fisch. *Principles of Problem Formation and Problem Resolution.* New York: Norton, 1974.

Wegscheider, S. *Another Chance: Hope and Health for the Alcoholic Family.* Palo Alto, CA: Science and Behavior Books, 1981.

Wood, P. E. *How to Get Yourself to Do What You Want to Do.* Englewood Cliffs, NJ: Prentice-Hall, 1976.

York, P., D. York, and T. Wachtel. *Toughlove.* Garden City, NY: Doubleday, 1982.

Zackon, F., W. E. McAuliffe, and J. M. N. Ch'ien. *Addict Aftercare: Recovery Training and Self-help.* (DHHS Pub. No. (ADM) 85–1341). Washington, D.C.: U.S. Government Printing Office, 1985.

Notes

1. THE FAMILY PERSPECTIVE

1. C. A. Eldred and M. N. Washington, "Interpersonal Relationships in Heroin Use By Men and Women and Their Role in Treatment Outcome," *International Journal of the Addictions 11* (1976): 117–130.
2. J. D. Miller and I. H. Cisin, *Highlights from the National Survey on Drug Abuse,* DHHS Pub. No. (ADM) 83–1277 (Washington, D.C.: U.S. Government Printing Office, 1982).
3. D. Waldorf and P. Biernacki, "The Natural Recovery from Opiate Addiction: Some Preliminary Findings," *Journal of Drug Issues 11* (1981): 61–74.
4. J. C. Ball and R. W. Snarr, "A Test of the Maturation Hypothesis with Respect to Opiate Addiction," *Bulletin on Narcotics 21* (1969): 9–13.
5. E. Kaufman, *Substance Abuse and Family Therapy* (New York: Grune & Stratton, 1985).

2. HOW DRUG ABUSE HAPPENS IN FAMILIES

1. H. Milkman and W. Frosch, "Theory of Drug Use," in D. J. Lettieri, M. Sayers, and H. W. Pearson, eds., *Theories on Drug Abuse: Selected Contemporary Perspectives,* DHHS Pub. No (ADM) 80–967 (Washington, D.C.: U.S. Government Printing Office, 1980).
2. C. A. Dackis and M. S. Gold, "Opiate Addiction and Depression: Cause or Effect?" *Drug and Alcohol Dependence 11* (1983): 105–109.
3. A considerable body of knowledge indicates that drug abuse by a family member can hold the family together. This point of view is summarized in a review by H. T. Harbin and H. M. Maziar, "The Families of Drug Abusers: A Literature Review," *Family Process 14* (1975): 411–431.
4. B. Levy, "Five Years After: A Follow-up of 50 Narcotic Addicts," *American Journal of Psychiatry 7* (1972): 102–106.

3. STAGES OF FAMILY LIFE AND DRUG ABUSE

1. M.A. Solomon, "A Developmental Conceptual Premise for Family Therapy," *Family Process 12* (1973): 179–183.
2. Ibid.
3. E. Carter and M. McGoldrick, *The Family Life Cycle: A Conceptual Framework for Family Therapy* (New York: Gardner Press, 1980).
4. M. Karpel and E. Strauss, *Family Evaluation* (New York: Gardner Press, 1983).
5. S. Coleman, J. D. Kaplan, and R. W. Downing, "Life Cycle and Loss: The Spiritual Vacuum of Heroin Addiction," *Family Process 25* (1986): 5–23.

6. I. Boszormenyi-Nagy and G. Spark, *Invisible Loyalties: Reciprocity in Intergenerational Family Therapy* (New York: Brunner/Mazel, 1984).

4. FAMILY PATTERNS ACROSS GENERATIONS

1. M. Bowen, *Family Therapy in Clinical Practice* (New York: Jason Aronson, 1978).
2. M. McGoldrick and R. Gerson. *Genograms in Family Assessment* (New York: W. W. Norton, 1985).
3. G. Bernal, C. Dragin, Y. Flores-Ortiz, and G. Diamond, *Intergenerational Family Therapy—Manual,* unpublished manuscript (San Francisco: University of California, San Francisco at San Francisco General Hospital, 1985).
4. The family tree is one way to learn about a family's roots. However, there are a number of other ways to find out the same information. For example, genealogists have been doing this kind of work for a long time and from a somewhat different perspective. For the genealogist, the important point remains to uncover the past and learn about oneself. There are a number of genealogical organizations that can help in the search for family information. In Chapter 10 we include some of this information along with a number of tips and suggestions on how to search for family roots.
5. I. Boszormenyi-Nagy and G. Spark, *Invisible Loyalties: Reciprocity in Intergenerational Family Therapy* (New York: Harper & Row, 1973).
6. D. Stanton, T. Todd, and Associates, *The Family Therapy of Drug Abuse and Addiction* (New York: Guilford Press, 1982).
7. Ibid.
8. Boszormenyi-Nagy and Spark, *Invisible Loyalties*
9. Ibid.
10. Stanton, *et al. The Family Therapy of Drug Abuse.*
11. G. Bernal and A. I. Alvarez, "Culture and Class in the Study of the Family," in C. Falicov, ed., *Cultural Perspectives in Family Therapy* (Rockville, MD.: Aspyn Systems Press, 1983).
12. E. Kaufman, *Substance Abuse and Family Therapy* (New York: Grune & Stratton, 1985).

5. HOW A FAMILY PERSPECTIVE CAN HELP

1. G. Bernal, "Parentification and Deparentification in Family Therapy," in A. S. Gurman, ed., *Questions and Answers in Family Therapy,* Vol. 2 (New York: Brunner/Mazel, 1982).
2. P. Watzlawick, J. Weakland, and R. Fisch, *Principles of Problem Formation and Problem Resolution* (New York: Norton, 1974).
3. I. Boszormenyi-Nagy and G. Spark, *Invisible Loyalties: Reciprocity in Intergenerational Family Therapy* (New York: Harper & Row, 1973).
4. G. Bernal and S. Baker, "Toward a Meta-communicational Framework for Couple Interactions. *Family Process 18* (1979): 293–302.
5. Ibid.

6. SAYING "NO" TO DRUGS AND BUILDING MOTIVATION

1. For more information on saying "no," see the following: M. J. Smith, *When I Say No I Feel Guilty: How to Cope—Using the Skills of Systematic Assertive Therapy* (New York: Dial Press, 1975); R. E. Alberti and M. L. Emmons, *Your Perfect Right: A Guide to Assertive Training,* 4th ed. (San Luis Obispo, CA: Impact Publishers, 1982); S. A. Bower and G. H. Bower, *Asserting Yourself: A Practical Guide for Positive Change* (Reading, MA: Addison-Wesley, 1976); and P. E. Wood, *How to Get Yourself to Do What You Want to Do* (Englewood Cliffs, NJ: Prentice-Hall, 1976).
2. For a detailed explanation of problem-solving models, see G. Emery, *A New Beginning: How You Can Change Your Life Through Cognitive Therapy* (New York: Simon and Schuster, 1981); and M. Mahoney, *Self-change: Strategies for Solving Personal Problems* (New York: Norton, 1979).
3. D.A. Darten, *Quitting: Knowing When to Leave* (New York: Walker and Company, 1980).

7. RECOGNIZING THE SIGNS OF DRUG ABUSE

1. S. Cohen, *The Substance Abuse Problems* (New York: Haworth Press, 1981).
2. E. M. Brecher, *Licit and Illicit Drugs* (Boston: Little, Brown, and Co., 1972).
3. W.A. Allen, N. L. Piccone, and D. D'Amanda, *How Drugs Can Affect Your Life* (Springfield, IL: Charles C. Thomas, 1983).
4. N. A. Cummings, "Turning Bread into Stones: Our Modern Antimiracle," *American Psychologist 34* (1979): 1119–1129.

8. TREATMENT ALTERNATIVES

1. H. Briggs, "Conference on Self-help and Health: Summary of Discussion," in A. Gartner and F. Riessman, eds., *Self-help and Health: A Report* (New York: Queens College, City University of New York, 1976).
2. M. Rose, R. Battjes, and C. Leukfeld, *Family Life Skills Training for Drug Abuse Prevention,* DHHS Pub. No. (ADM) 84–1340 (Washington, D.C.: U.S. Government Printing Office, 1984).
3. J. D. Baron, *Kids and Drugs: A Parent's Handbook of Drug Abuse Prevention and Treatment* (New York: GD/Perigee Books, 1981).
4. P. York, D. York, and T. Wachtel, *Toughlove.* (Garden City, NY: Doubleday, 1982).
5. M. Manatt, *Parents, Peers, and Pot,* DHHS Pub. No. (ADM) 81–812 (Washington, D.C.: U.S. Government Printing Office, 1979).
6. M. Manatt, *Parents, Peers, and Pot II: Parents in Action,* DHHS Pub. No. (ADM) 83–1290 (Washington, D.C.: U.S. Government Printing Office, 1983).
7. D. N. Nurco and N. Wegner, *Manual for Working with Parents of Adolescent Drug Users,* DHHS Pub. No. (ADM) 83–1209 (Washington, D.C.: U.S. Government Printing Office, 1982).
8. D. Nurco, N. Wegner, P. Stephenson, A. Makofsky, and J. W. Shaffer, *Ex-addicts' Self-help Groups: Potentials and Pitfalls* (New York: Praeger, 1983).

9. J. M. N. Ch'ien, "Alumni Associations of Hong Kong," in B. S. Brown, ed., *Addicts and Aftercare* (Beverly Hills: Sage Publications, 1979), 155–163.

10. F. Zackon, W. E. McAuliffe, and J. M. N. Ch'ien, *Addict Aftercare: Recovery Training and Self-help,* DHHS Pub. No. (ADM) 85–1341 (Washington, D.C.: U.S. Government Printing Office, 1985).

11. Nurco, *et al. Ex-addicts' Self-Help Groups.*

12. D. N. Nurco, P. Stephenson, and L. Naesea, *Manual for Setting Up Self-help Groups of Ex-narcotic Addicts,* DHHS Pub. No. (ADM) 81–1087 (Washington, D.C.: U.S. Government Printing Office, 1981).

13. S. Wegscheider, *Another Chance: Hope and Health for the Alcoholic Family* (Palo Alto, CA: Science and Behavior Books, 1981).

14. Rose, *et al. Family Life Skills.*

15. B. Guerney, *Relationship Enhancement: Skill-training Programs for Therapy, Problem Prevention, and Enrichment* (San Francisco: Jossey-Bass, 1977).

16. L. L'Abate, *Enrichment: Structured Interventions with Couples, Families, and Groups* (Washington, D.C.: University Press of America, 1977).

17. J. Szapocznik, D. Santisteban, W. Kurtines, A. Perez-Vidal, and O. Hervis, *Bicultural Effectiveness Training* (Miami: University of Miami Spanish Family Guidance Center, 1982).

18. G. Bernal, J. L. Sorensen, R. Wortman, and L. Wermuth, *Psychoeducational Training: A Manual for Family Members and Sponsors of Methadone Maintenance Patients* (San Francisco: University of California, San Francisco Substance Abuse Services, 1985).

19. A. M. Cruze, H. J. Harwood, P. L. Kristiansen, J. J. Collins, and D. C. Jones, *Economic Costs to Society of Alcohol and Drug Abuse and Mental Illness—1977,* DHHS Pub. No. (ADM) 81–1179 (Washington, D.C.: U.S. Government Printing Office, 1977).

20. J. C. Ball, L. Rosen, J. A. Flueck, and D. N. Nurco, "Lifetime Criminality of Heroin Addicts in the United States," *Journal of Drug Issues 12* (1982): 225–239.

21. J. Newmeyer, G. Johnson, and S. Klot, "Acupuncture as a Detoxification Modality," *Journal of Psychoactive Drugs 16* (1984): 241–261.

22. F. Klajner, L. M. Hartman, and M. B. Sobell, "Treatment of Substance Abuse by Relaxation Training: A Review of Its Rationale, Efficacy, and Mechanisms." *Addictive Behaviors 9* (1984): 41–55.

23. P. J. DuPont and L. A. Jason, "Assertiveness Training in a Preventive Drug Education Program," *Journal of Drug Education 14* (1984): 369–378.

9. AIDS, DRUG ABUSE, AND THE FAMILY

1. B. G. Faltz and S. Madover, "AIDS, Drugs, and Alcohol: The Connection," in M. Helquist, ed., *Living with AIDS* (Los Angeles: AIDS Project Los Angeles, in press).

2. D. C. Des Jarlais, S. R. Friedman, and D. Strug, "AIDS and Needle Sharing within the IV Drug Use Subculture," in D. Feldman and T. Johnson, eds., *The Social Dimensions of AIDS: Methods and Theory* (New York: Praeger, in press).

3. Centers for Infectious Diseases, *Acquired Immunodeficiency Syndrome (AIDS) Weekly Surveillance Report: United States AIDS Activity* (Atlanta: Centers for Disease Control, November 18, 1985).

4. M. F. Rogers, "AIDS in Children: A Review of the Clinical, Epidemiologic, and Public Health Aspects," *Pediatric Infectious Diseases 4* (1985): 230–236.
5. D. C. Des Jarlais, "AIDS Among Intravenous Drug Users: Overview and Update," presented at the International Conference on AIDS, Atlanta, Georgia (April 1985).
6. R. E. Chaisson, R. Onishi, A. R. Moss, D. Osmond, and J. R. Carlson, "Risks of HTLV-III/LAV Infection in Heterosexual Intravenous Drug Abusers in San Francisco," presented at the International Conference on AIDS, Paris, France (June 1986); and R. D'Aquila, A. B. Williams, H. D. Kleber, and A. E. Williams, "Prevalence of HTLV-III Infection Among New Haven, Connecticut, Parenteral Drug Abusers in 1982–83 [Correspondence]," *New England Journal of Medicine 314* (1986): 117–118.
7. G. H. Friedland, et al., "Lack of Transmission of HTLV-III/LAV Infection to Household Contacts of Patients with AIDS or AIDS Related Complex with Oral Candidiasis," *New England Journal of Medicine* 314 (1986): 344–349.
8. M. Marmor, D. C. Des Jarlais, S. R. Friedman, M. Lyden, and W. El-Sadr, "The Epidemic of Acquired Immunodeficiency Syndrome (AIDS) and Suggestions for Its Control in Drug Abusers," *Journal of Substance Abuse Treatment 1* (1984): 237–247; and E. Drucker, "AIDS and Addiction in New York City," *American Journal of Drug and Alcohol Abuse 12* (1986): 165–181.

Index